GILBERT AND SULLIVAN

WILLIAM S. GILBERT

ARTHUR S. SULLIVAN

GILBERT

AND

SULLIVAN

BY

NORMAN WYMER

PORTRAITS BY JOHN PIMLOTT

E. P. DUTTON & CO., INC.

NEW YORK

First published in the U.S.A. 1963
by E. P. Dutton & Co., Inc.

Copyright © 1962 by Norman Wymer
All rights reserved. Printed in the U.S.A.

FIRST EDITION

927
G 466

Library of Congress Catalog Card Number: 63-8597

The author has based this portrait of Gilbert and Sullivan upon the personal correspondence and other documents of his two subjects; upon the various full-length biographies that have been published since their death; upon original researches of contemporary reports in *The Times* and other newspapers; and upon first-hand information supplied to him many years ago by one of the most popular of the original Gilbert and Sullivan players, Jessie Bond, whom he interviewed on several occasions during the years of her retirement.

Much of the dialogue contained in this book is recounted in the actual words of Gilbert or Sullivan, and, where this has not been possible, it is founded on factual evidence.

N.W.

In indicating the sums of money paid Gilbert and Sullivan, we have used the pre-World War II rate of five dollars to the British pound.—Editor

Contents

GILBERT AND SULLIVAN

CHAPTER ONE

The Early Years of W. S. Gilbert

One fine sunny day in the early spring of 1839 William Gilbert was toddling beside his nurse in Naples, on his morning walk, when two charming Italians ran up to them from behind and told the nurse they had been sent by the child's father, a retired naval surgeon, to fetch "Bab" home again. "A gentleman has called and wishes to see the boy," they explained, puffing.

"But who—who are you?" stuttered the nurse in surprise. "I don't know you! I have never seen either of you before!"

"Do not be alarmed, *Signorita*. You can trust us!" the Italians assured her.

Smiling disarmingly, they gave a half-bow and whisked William away before the nurse had the chance to resist. They led the small boy through the mean back streets of Naples, passing many beggars on the pavements, to the outskirts of the town. There, they mounted a donkey cart and jogged into the countryside, through rich vineyards and olive plantations, to a lonely chalet in the Apennines Mountains.

When the nurse returned to the Gilberts' villa, she was horrified to find that Bab had not arrived. When she weepingly explained what had happened, William's peppery father turned on her in fury. "The child has been kidnaped, and all through your stupidity!" he fumed.

His mother had hysterics and kept wailing that Bab would be killed.

"There's only one thing to do—report the matter to the police immediately!" snapped the naval surgeon, springing from his chair.

At that moment, there was a knock at the front door. They all caught their breath, hoping that this might be Bab, but the caller proved to be a messenger with a note from the kidnapers, demanding a ransom for the boy's safe return. William's father, fearing that his son might come to harm if he were to refuse, angrily paid the ransom; and a few hours later Bab was deposited safely on his doorstep, his kidnapers giving one loud knock to announce his return and then fleeing before the door could be opened.

William, who was only two, was in high spirits as, in his childish way, he prattled about his adventures to his parents: far from being afraid, he had found it exciting to be taken into the mysterious mountains by strange men. He remembered his kidnaping vividly all his life; and many years later the incident was to give him the idea for one of the most popular of the Gilbert and Sullivan operas, *The Pirates of Penzance.*

William's parents were restless people, and it was for this reason that he was taken to Naples. The Gilberts had a comfortable house at Hammersmith—then only a village, on the outskirts of London—but they seldom lived there for more than a few months at a time. Their marriage was not a happy one, and they shared so few interests in common that they grew bored with each other's company and bickered eternally unless they were constantly on the move. And so, for the sake of harmony, they spent most of their time traveling in Europe with William and his three sisters. At the age of seven, William, a good-looking boy and tall for his age, began to attend a small day school at Boulogne, but before he had learned very much he was taken away again as his parents decided to stay in another part of France. Always they were on the move.

William hated this roving life. "If only we could have our own home like other children!" he would complain to his sisters.

His sisters felt the same way. "We've no one to play with—no *real* friends!"

All four children were already beginning to notice their parents' edginess toward each other, and this made them very unhappy. William was especially conscious of their discord.

Even so, he was lucky to have the opportunity of visiting other countries. One day, during a visit to Paris, William, by now in his teens, had an unexpected thrill when the Emperor Napoleon III and the Empress Eugénie passed in procession along the Champs Elysées and appeared to smile at him. William's head had recently been shaved, following an attack of typhoid fever, but, instead of being sensitive about his bald scalp, he was rather proud of it because it made him different from other people. Being rather self-opinionated, he felt sure the Emperor and Empress must be discussing him to his advantage; and so, on returning to the family's apartments, he got out his notebook and pencil and composed a verse about their imaginary conversation:

> To the Emperor she said:
> "How beautiful the head
> Of that youth of gallant mien,
> Cropped so neat and close and clean—
> Though I own he's rather lean."

Said the Emperor: "It is!
And I never saw a phiz
More wonderful than 'is!"

Already Gilbert was showing a gift for writing humorous verse, as well as for drawing. He loved reading, too. But his education had been badly neglected. It was beginning to look as if he might never receive any formal schooling, when suddenly his parents grew as bored with traveling as they had been with staying at home, and decided to settle permanently in England. The Gilberts returned to their house at Hammersmith, and William was sent to a school at Ealing where Thackeray, Captain Frederick Marryat and several other famous men had been taught.

Having mixed so seldom with other boys, Gilbert took an immediate dislike to school life, with its irritating rules and regimentation, and he made himself very unpopular by showing an aggressive resentment of the discipline. His restless and unhappy childhood had made him oversensitive and quick to take offense, self-assertive and cantankerous. If another boy crossed him, Gilbert would fly into a tantrum and punch his head. Being tall and powerfully built, he did not mind whom he fought, nor what the consequences: he would lash out at the prefects if they tried to thwart him.

Gilbert also exasperated his masters by his laziness. Though he had a good brain, he hated lessons and refused to exert himself, until his headmaster summoned him to his study for a reprimand. "Gilbert, you are a disgrace to the school and to your parents!" ranted the headmaster, pacing angrily up and down the room. "Every week you rank below boys of less brain than yourself, simply on account of your idleness."

This remark cut Gilbert, who flushed with indignation. Secretly, he considered himself the cleverest boy in the school—a genius, in fact—and he was filled with sudden shame and anger at the thought of his "inferiors" beating him in class. Determined to prove his brilliance, he at last began to put his back into his work. He ended the term at the top of his form and won two or three prizes, but he still had to be prodded from time to time to keep him up to the mark.

As he rose in the school, Gilbert developed another field for self-expression—composing witty verses, with unkind caricatures, about both boys and masters. For this offense, he had to pay many visits to the headmaster.

"I presume this is also your work, Gilbert?" his headmaster snorted, handing him a verse about himself.

"Yes, sir," Gilbert admitted.

"Just so! Well, what have you to say for yourself this time?"

Gilbert scanned through the verse and frowned. "I'm ashamed, sir! I . . ."

"H'm! It is about time you showed some shame!" the headmaster grunted.

Gilbert gave an impish smile. "I was going to say, sir," he continued, "that I'm ashamed of the *quality* of the verse! It is really very trivial! I can certainly write far better than that, sir."

The headmaster glowered. "You will do well, Gilbert, to direct your talents into a more worthy field!" he snapped, and dismissed him from his study.

While continuing to compose his verses, Gilbert soon began to turn his talents to writing playlets, which he produced at school with a cast of boys. This led to more fighting, for, if a member of his cast failed to obey his stage instructions to the letter, Gilbert would promptly exercise his authority by striking the culprit.

In one play, about Guy Fawkes and the Gunpowder Plot, Gilbert himself acted one of the principal parts, and drew high praise from his masters. This fired his imagination. Believing himself to have the makings of a great actor, he had a sudden whim to make the stage his career, and a few days later, without a word to anyone, he played truant from school and made his way to the Haymarket Theatre in the hope of persuading the famous actor Charles Kean to give him a job.

Young Gilbert bounced into the theater with his usual self-assurance, but, when confronted by Kean, he was overawed by the actor's strong personality and powerful voice, and became practically speechless.

"So you want to be an actor—eh?" Kean roared.

"Ye-yes," stuttered Gilbert.

"How old are you?"

"F-fifteen, s-sir."

"Fifteen, eh? You're tall for your age! What are you doing now?"

Gilbert reddened and tried to dodge the question.

"What are you doing now, eh?" Kean repeated, fixing the boy with his penetrating eye.

"I—I'm still at school," Gilbert said sheepishly.

Kean grunted and asked his name. Unfortunately for Gilbert, Kean happened to know his father, and he was unwilling to take any action without first consulting him. When Gilbert confessed that he had run away from school to become an actor without his father's knowledge, Kean abruptly closed the interview and sent him straight back to school.

With constant prodding by his masters, Gilbert rose to be head of the school, and then went on to take a degree at London University, completing his education at the age of nineteen.

By now he had lost his ambition to become an actor. Indeed, he had no ambition to be anything in particular. His bent was for writing and drawing, and he could see no prospect of earning his living from these sources. As the Crimean War was now being fought, he decided to obtain a commission in the army, but, before he made application, the Russians surrendered at Sevastopol and the war ended. Whereupon Gilbert lost interest in soldiering, though later he joined the militia. Since no more attractive opportunity presented itself, he finally became a clerk in the education department of the Privy Council, for which he received a salary of £120 ($600) a year.

He disliked his job every bit as much as he had disliked school. The monotonous routine and rigid regulations, so stifling to initiative, got on his nerves. And so did his colleagues. He thought them colorless and would try to shake them out of their rut by playing practical jokes, which, however, merely infuriated them.

After he had stuck with the job for four years, doing as little work as possible, an aunt died and unexpectedly left Gilbert a legacy of £400 ($2,000). On the day he received this good news, Gilbert went beamingly to the head of his department, and impulsively informed him: "Sir, I have been left a fortune. I wish to resign my post."

"Good, Gilbert—splendid!" his chief replied, his attention focused on a new sheaf of government orders.

"Yes, sir—it was a great surprise. An aunt . . ."

"I am not referring to your fortune, Gilbert. I refer to your leaving this office!"

"Oh!"

"Yes," his chief went on, still studying his papers, "I am delighted to hear of your resignation as it will save me the possible embarrassment of having to give you notice!"

Gilbert certainly had not expected this reception, though later, on looking back, he saw the justification and good-humoredly described his employment at the Privy Council as "one of the worst bargains any government ever made."

Gilbert, by now a strapping young man of over six feet, decided to spend his "fortune" on qualifying in law and setting up in practice as a barrister (lawyer). For his first case, he was briefed to prosecute a slovenly Irish woman, charged with stealing a coat. Rising sedately, Gilbert glanced around in the professional manner, fingered his wig, and proceeded to address the judge: "May it please your lordship, I . . ." But the prisoner allowed him to say no more.

"Ah, ye devil—sit down!" she suddenly screamed from the dock. "Don't listen to him, yer honor! He's a drunkard! He's known in all the pubs! . . . Sit down, yer drunkard!"

Every time Gilbert tried to open his mouth, she hurled more abuse at him. In desperation, he appealed to the recorder to restore order, but the recorder, like everyone else, was convulsed with laughter and incapable of intervention. Controlling his temper with difficulty, Gilbert finally shouted above the uproar, and the woman was sentenced to three months' imprisonment.

Gilbert's next case proved still more disastrous. This time he appeared for the defense, and his own client turned on him. He was briefed to defend a woman of respectable appearance who was charged with stealing a purse from a passenger on a bus. The purse had been found by the police in the pocket of her coat, but the woman assured Gilbert that it had been planted there by somebody else—by the real thief. As his client always carried a hymnbook on her and appeared to be deeply religious, Gilbert did not think it necessary to inquire too closely into her character: he decided to pursue her line of defense and felt sure he would obtain her acquittal.

"Now tell me, my man," he patronizingly asked the police witness in cross-examination, "did you find anything else in this good lady's pocket apart from the purse?"

"Yes, sir, I did."

"Oh! And what did you find?" Gilbert asked.

The policeman looked at his notebook and stiffened. "I found two other purses, a watch, two silver pencils and, er, a hymnbook," he told Gilbert triumphantly.

A gale of laughter swept the court.

Gilbert, clearly flustered, ordered the policeman to step down, and requested the crier to call the witnesses who had promised to bear testimony to his client's good character. "Call witnesses! Call witnesses!" the crier shouted in the corridors outside. But not a single person came forward.

"Dear me, dear me, this is unfortunate—really most unfortunate!" Gilbert muttered. "They must have mistaken the day!" Covered with confusion, he turned to the judge and mumbled a request for an adjournment of the case, but the judge refused this. Instead, he proceeded to pass judgment, sentencing the prisoner to eighteen months' hard labor.

At this, the prisoner lost her temper with her counsel for his mishandling of her case. In a flash, she whipped off her boot and hurled it across the court at Gilbert's head with a storm of abusive language that was most unexpected in a woman of her pretensions.

Gilbert was certainly a most incompetent lawyer— casual to his clients, careless over the preparation of his briefs, and a very bad orator, who easily became flustered and irritable when a case appeared to be going against him. Indeed, there was so little to commend him that his services were seldom sought. During his first two years as a lawyer, he earned only about £25 ($125).

Clearly, Gilbert was unlikely to make his fortune in law. He must quickly find some other source of revenue —or starve.

CHAPTER TWO

Gilbert Becomes a Writer

Instead of idly waiting for clients who never came, Gilbert now bought himself a new quill, a large sheaf of paper and a drawing block, and tried to make ends meet by turning his gifts for writing and drawing to profit as a spare-time occupation.

He wrote illustrated articles on various topics and submitted these to the leading weekly magazines in complete confidence that they would be accepted, but each was returned to him within a few days with the editor's regrets that it was not up to publication standard. Gilbert bristled with indignation. "This is ridiculous!" he exploded when the twelfth of his manuscripts shot back through his mailbox. "My articles are much better than most that are published—very much better! The editors are fools—not fit for their jobs!"

Refusing to accept their decisions as final, Gilbert decided to bludgeon his way into print. He went straight to his writing table, took up his quill, and wrote to the owners of the magazines concerned telling them of the stupidity of their editors in not appreciating his genius, and asking them to give his articles their personal consideration—and his bold and highhanded tactics met with surprising success. Several of the magazine owners saw that

Gilbert indeed showed talent, and instructed their editors to publish his work.

Though resentful at having their decisions overruled, these editors hesitated to reject any further articles by Gilbert, who before long was earning considerably more from his free-lance journalism than from his fees as a barrister. The prospect of his earning his living by writing alone still seemed very remote, however, until a new humorous magazine called *Fun* appeared on the bookstalls.

Here's my chance, thought Gilbert as he studied a copy of the first issue. This is the magazine for me—just the type I could write for!

Acting upon a sudden inspiration, he sat down and wrote an amusing illustrated feature about some topic of the day and sent this direct to the owner of *Fun,* who found it so entertaining that he passed on the manuscript to his editor with the recommendation to engage Gilbert as a regular contributor. "This young man shows real wit and may well go far," he predicted.

A few days later, Gilbert, to his surprise and delight, received an invitation to call on the editor at his shabby office behind a glassware shop in a London back street. The editor received him most affably—almost as though Gilbert were already an established author. "Ah, good morning, Mr. Gilbert, good morning! Pray be seated," he invited him, drawing up a chair with the stuffing poking through the seat. "I have read your article with much amusement. Indeed, I would go so far as to say that I consider it outstanding, quite outstanding."

Gilbert was of the same opinion, but replied with false modesty: "Oh, it's really very trivial—just an idea that occurred to me!"

The editor stroked his chin. "H'm! Tell me, do you often get ideas of this nature?" he asked.

"Oh, I usually manage to find something amusing to jot down," Gilbert replied, trying to appear casual.

"Good! Then I would like you to write for me regularly," the editor told him.

Gilbert beamed with satisfaction as he recalled the pile of rejection slips that had greeted his first attempts at writing.

"What I want," the editor continued, "is something really amusing—something original such as you will not find in other magazines. I give you a free hand to write what you like—provided, of course, that you keep strictly within the bounds of propriety!"

This was a most important condition because most people's views on propriety were very much stricter in Victorian times than nowadays, and their sense of humor was considerably narrower and less flexible than ours. Many things that we consider funny the Victorians would not have thought at all amusing, and consequently literature of a humorous nature tended to be very staid.

Gilbert, having an unusually keen sense of humor and also a vivid imagination, could see a funny side to this prim and proper Victorian life, and he decided to break new ground in his literary work by poking fun at it, though without taking liberties that might cause offense. He decided to create in comic verse a world of fantasy, based on real life: a world of *Topsy-Turvydom*—

> The other night, from cares exempt,
> I slept—and what do you think I dreamt?
> I dreamt that somehow I had come
> To dwell in Topsy-Turvydom!—
> Where vice is virtue—virtue, vice:
> Where nice is nasty—nasty, nice:
> Where right is wrong and wrong is right—
> Where white is black and black is white.

By ridiculing his fellow men, Gilbert was exposing himself to the possibility of ridicule. He was taking a risk that might either make or mar his prospects as a writer, but he knew just how far it was safe to go. He skillfully framed his verses to allow his readers to laugh at others without also having to laugh at themselves. Since he gave no one cause to feel personally affronted, his readers found Gilbert's wit highly entertaining, and a most refreshing change from the sedate humor to which they were accustomed. People began to quote his verses, and to parody them. Indeed, Gilbert's new brand of humor proved so popular that it later became know as "Gilbertian," and a collection of his verses, most of which had a topical twist, was published in book form under the title of *The Bab Ballads*—a book that now ranks as a classic.

The editor of *Fun,* finding his sales soaring beyond his highest hopes, kept pressing Gilbert to add to the number of his contributions. "I want more verses, more articles—double the number!" he told him.

Gilbert protested that he was running dry of ideas, but the editor brushed aside his objections. "Never mind, never mind, new ideas will soon come to you! Write about anything!"

Gilbert wrote about everything and nothing, and it all made amusing reading. He received very small pay for his contributions—no more than a pound (about $5) per column—but his prospects seemed so promising that, at the age of twenty-seven, he finally decided to abandon law and to make writing his profession. He had by then been a barrister for four years, during which time he had received perhaps twenty briefs and earned little more than £100 ($500). Nevertheless, those years were not fruitless because his unfortunate experiences at the bar, like his kidnaping at Naples, were later to give Gilbert the inspiration and material for another comic opera, *Trial by Jury*.

It was soon after he became a professional journalist that Gilbert began to turn his attention to writing for the stage. Though he no longer felt any wish to act, he was still captivated by the theater, and he therefore persuaded the editor of *Fun* to appoint him the magazine's drama critic, in addition to his other activities. He threw himself into theatrical circles with keen enthusiasm, making friends with actors, dramatists and producers.

Every Saturday evening, on leaving the theater, Gilbert and some six to a dozen dramatists and critics would meet at his rooms for a dinner of steak pie, cold boiled beef, Stilton cheese, and a generous quantity of ale. Gay and carefree, they would sit over their tankards of ale until the early hours of the morning, laughing, singing and cracking jokes. But no jokes could match Gilbert's more subtle witticisms. Again and again, he would set the party rollicking by some brilliant flash of humor. "Really, Gilbert, you are incorrigible!" his companions would splutter, mopping their tears of laughter.

As a result of these parties, Gilbert came to form a close friendship with Tom Robertson, who, though not much older than himself, was already achieving recognition as one of the leading dramatists and producers of the day. Gilbert began to accompany Robertson to the theater to watch his methods of play production, and it was not long before he was expressing an ambition to try his hand at writing plays himself. "I don't want to spend my life scribbling verse," he confided to his friend. "I mean, it's all so trivial—pure nonsense, really!"

"Ah, but clever nonsense!" Robertson chuckled.

"Yes, yes," Gilbert retorted impatiently, "I know I have a knack for verse, and, of course, I shall continue to write it, but I also feel capable of something better! I want to produce work of greater literary merit—work that will make my name."

"And you think plays may bring you fame," Robertson put in.

"Exactly! . . . What do you think of my prospects?" Gilbert asked.

"Excellent, my dear chap, excellent! A man of your gifts could write anything," Robertson assured him. "Go to it, and good luck!"

Gilbert wrote some twenty plays during the next two years or so, but every one was rejected—just as his first articles had been. He began to despair. But then, in December 1866, two weeks or so after his thirtieth birthday, he received a letter from Miss Herbert, who leased the St. James's Theatre, in London, asking him to call on her immediately to discuss a proposition.

Gilbert bundled himself into his overcoat and went straight to the theater.

"I have sent for you at the suggestion of Mr. Tom Robertson," Miss Herbert explained with a genial smile. "I have often read your verse, but Mr. Robertson tells me that you are now writing plays as well."

Gilbert gaped. "Well, I . . . well, yes—yes, I am," he stuttered.

"Good! Then I think you can help me," Miss Herbert went on. "The fact is, Mr. Gilbert, I'm in a bit of a fix. I have no suitable play to produce for the Christmas season —nothing sufficiently lighthearted. I was wondering if you would care to write me a burlesque."

"What—in time for Christmas? But that's less than three weeks away!" Gilbert protested.

Miss Herbert smiled apologetically. "I know I'm not giving you much time, but Mr. Robertson says he's sure you can do it—if you will."

Gilbert required no more persuading. He settled to the task immediately and wrote a burlesque, *Dulcamara,* in less than a week. After only ten days of skimpy rehearsals, it was produced at the St. James's Theatre on December 29, and was received with acclaim.

In the hustle to get the play produced, one important point had been overlooked: no fee had been paid, or even suggested, to Gilbert for this work. A little hesitantly, he raised the matter with the manager of the theater's finances, who asked him how much he expected to receive.

Gilbert made a mental reckoning of the time and work involved and suggested thirty guineas, but the manager shook his head. "Oh, dear, no, we never pay in guineas. You must make it pounds," he bargained.

Gilbert accepted his offer with alacrity. He thought this a good bargain, until the manager, on handing him his check, observed: "Now take an old stager's advice— never sell so good a piece as this for £30 ($150) again."

He was indeed foolish, for *Dulcamara* had quite a long and profitable run. Gilbert, though smarting at his stupidity, thought that the play well deserved its success, but many years later, when he had grown more critical of his work, he went to watch a revival and considered it so bad that he hissed it from the auditorium. It was, in fact, an extremely indifferent play, but as it appealed to the theatergoers and critics alike, it established Gilbert as a playwright.

By now, Gilbert had fallen in love with the daughter of an army officer, Lucy Turner, an attractive fair-haired girl of nineteen—eleven years younger than himself— whom he nicknamed "Kitten," on account of her lively and happy disposition. Feeling himself now really on the ladder to fame, Gilbert celebrated the success of *Dulcamara* by marrying Lucy the following August. They went to

France for their honeymoon, Gilbert unromantically spending the journey writing another "Bab Ballad," and then settled in Kensington. Lucy proved a perfect wife. Charming and tactful, she knew how to humor her husband when he was moody or bad tempered, and, though she bore him no children, she gave him the happy home life for which he had always longed.

Gilbert, who was also a good husband, required a great deal of humoring during the first two or three years of their marriage, for his ladder to fame proved steeper than he had expected. In spite of the success of *Dulcamara,* he experienced the greatest difficulty in getting a second play accepted. He wrote at least a dozen new plays, and all were rejected almost by return mail. "I cannot understand it!" Gilbert expostulated, tossing his latest rejection onto the breakfast table. "These theatrical managers, they . . ."

"I know, dear, they are very trying!" his wife tactfully agreed, anticipating the rest of his sentence.

Gilbert snorted. "They return my manuscripts so quickly," he went on, "that they hardly give themselves time to read them!" He paused and then exclaimed as an afterthought: "I wonder if they do read them! I wonder."

He decided to put one manager to the test. He wrote a blank-verse play parodying Tennyson's poem *The Princess* and submitted this with several of the middle pages loosely gummed together. Back it came, in the same condition as he had dispatched it. So Gilbert decided to go into action. Like a dog with its hackles up, he stumped along to the theater and confronted the manager. "Why did you reject this play?" he growled.

The manager made the excuse that he had not considered it quite suitable for his audience.

"Did you read it?" snapped Gilbert.

The manager appeared hurt. "My dear Gilbert, how can you ask? Of course, I read it."

"By gum, you did *not!*" Gilbert almost shouted, holding the gummed pages up to the manager's eyes.

Again Gilbert's bludgeoning tactics were rewarded. The manager, forced to admit his guilt, reluctantly read the manuscript of *The Princess*—and accepted it. The play was produced early in 1870 and proved such a dazzling success that Gilbert was promoted to the front rank of British dramatists almost overnight.

His career was beginning to pan out just as he wished. But Gilbert had by now met Arthur Sullivan; and all his schemes were soon to be turned topsy-turvy.

CHAPTER THREE

The Early Years of Arthur Sullivan

Arthur Sullivan, who was about five years younger than Gilbert, had a very much happier childhood. His parents were devoted to one another and, though extremely poor, were willing to make sacrifices for their children, instead of always putting their own interests first, as the Gilberts did.

They had no social advantages such as the Gilberts enjoyed. Sullivan's father played the clarinet in a small theater orchestra for a wage of only about a pound a week, and it is said that his mother, who was of Italian origin, was accompanying an organ grinder and his monkey through the slums of South London when they met. After the birth of their first son, Frederick, Mrs. Sullivan, to help make ends meet, placed the child in the care of friends and took a temporary live-in job with a family, leaving her husband to fend for himself. "It's the only thing to do, but it's worth the sacrifice," they consoled each other.

While his wife was away, Mr. Sullivan struggled to earn some extra money by teaching in his spare time and then sitting up into the night copying music by candlelight. When he had managed to save a few pounds, they were reunited and rented a cheap terrace house in an alley leading off the Lambeth Walk.

It was in this shabby house, badly in need of repair and painting, that Arthur Sullivan was born, in May 1842. When he was three years old, his father was appointed bandmaster at the Royal Military College. This eased his financial worries a little, but nevertheless he still had to exercise the most rigid economy, denying himself and his family everything except the barest essentials.

The Sullivans, however, gave their children something that no money could buy—the love and tender care that bring real happiness. Frederick and Arthur returned their love, and, having sunny natures, found pleasure in the simplest things.

Their joy was great when one morning their father asked them: "How would you like to come with me to the band practice today?"

Arthur pranced with excitement.

Mr. Sullivan smiled and affectionately patted his head of thick, curly black hair. "Very well, I will let you sit in a corner of the music room while the band plays. But you must be very quiet," he warned them. "If I hear a sound from either of you, I shall send you out again immediately!"

Neither boy made a murmur. Arthur was enthralled by the various instruments, each so different and yet combining in perfect harmony, and, after the practice, he asked his father to teach him music.

Mr. Sullivan laughed good-naturedly. "You are too small, my boy! Why, some of the instruments are as big as yourself! One day, when you are older and have grown a bit, perhaps I will teach you," he added to placate him.

But Arthur Sullivan refused to be placated. A few days later, though he was only four, he crept into the music room when nobody was about, clambered onto the piano stool, and tried to teach himself music by striking the keys and making chords. His tuneful ear told him immediately which notes, when sounded together, were harmonious and which were discordant.

As he sat at the piano, his legs dangling in the air and his little hands stretching awkwardly along the keyboard, his father walked into the room. "Arthur, what are you doing? You know you are not allowed in here on your own!" he scolded him.

Arthur reddened. "I'm sorry, Father, I was only . . ."

Before he could say any more, Mr. Sullivan, who never could be really angry with his children, broke into a broad smile and squatted beside him on the piano stool to explain the various notes. Impressed by the boy's intelligence and enthusiasm during this short lesson, Mr. Sullivan decided to allow him into the music room at any time when it was not in use.

"But you must take the greatest care not to damage the piano," Mr. Sullivan told him.

"Oh, yes, Father, I will—the greatest care," the boy promised.

He went to the music room nearly every day thereafter. Though he was far too young to understand the technicalities of music, he memorized the notes and gradually discovered certain harmonic progressions, until, by the age of six, he had taught himself to play the piano by ear and to read scores that were not too complicated.

By this time, Frederick had also begun to learn music. Though he too was making good progress, he had not the talent of his younger brother, who now badgered his father to teach him the band instruments. "You said you would teach me when I was bigger, and I am much bigger now. Please, Father, *please!*" he pleaded in a captivating manner that always won people's hearts.

Mr. Sullivan, unable to resist his appeal, gave his son a few simple lessons on the clarinet and flute; and Arthur then set to work mastering these instruments with the same tenacity as he had taught himself the piano. From time to time, when he was not too busy with his own work, his father would go to the music room to give him a little help and encouragement. Surprised and delighted at the effortless ease with which the boy came to handle the clarinet, Mr. Sullivan gave him an unexpected reward. "My boy," he told him, "I have decided to let you play with the band."

Arthur gaped. "With the band, Father?"

Mr. Sullivan smiled proudly at his son. "Yes, my boy, you are doing so well that I am going to allow you to play the clarinet at today's practice."

Aglow with pride and joy, young Sullivan took his place with the smart uniformed bandsmen, who gave him amused smiles of encouragement when he raised his clarinet to his mouth. They imagined that his father was simply giving him a few minutes' treat, for it seemed impossible that anyone so young and small could have reached a sufficiently high standard to take part in a serious rehearsal with professional musicians. Arthur, however, surprised them by playing in perfect rhythm and without making any mistakes.

It was not long before he was taking part in the band practices regularly. The more he played, the more music meant to him. During the next two years or so, Sullivan patiently taught himself the rest of the wind instruments in the military band—the oboe, bassoon, horn, cornet, trombone and euphonium. He also learned how to write music for an orchestra, and even tried his hand at composing an anthem.

At the age of eight, Arthur Sullivan made the great decision of his life. "Father," he announced, "I want to be a musician like you."

This was no surprise to Mr. Sullivan, but, proud though he felt, he did not want his son to follow in his footsteps.

"Ah, my boy," he said, "you may love music but you do not know the terrible struggle a musician has to face to earn his living."

"It is a very hard life, Arthur," his mother added her warning. "Even the greatest musicians seldom make much money."

But Sullivan stood his ground. "I don't mind how little money I make as long as I can have music. I want to be a musician and nothing else," he declared.

His parents, realizing that this was not simply childish impetuosity, hesitated at first. Pleased as they were that he loved music, they thought of their own long struggles, and wanted to save their son from similar hardships. By constant scrimping and scraping, they had by now managed to save a little capital, and so they decided to spend part of this on sending him to a boarding school at Bayswater, in London, in the hope that this might broaden his outlook and lead to his choosing a career with better financial prospects. He was still very young, and there was plenty of time for him to change his mind.

Unlike Gilbert, Sullivan, though a delicate boy, entered into school life in a cheerful spirit and made himself extremely popular with everyone. He disliked lessons, however, just as much as Gilbert did. The only subject that held any interest for him was chemistry, where he could made "stinks and bangs." His heart was in music and nothing else.

When he had been at school for nearly four years, a chance incident occurred that was to carry him a long way toward his goal. While out for a walk with some of his friends, Sullivan met and got into conversation with a maid in the employ of the Rev. Thomas Helmore, master of the choristers of the Chapel Royal, St. James's.

"If you like music so much, you should live in our

house," the maid told him. "There you would have music every day."

"Music every day!" Arthur echoed in wonderment.

"They say that many great musicians began as choristers at the Chapel Royal," the maid went on.

Sullivan's eyes lit up. "Who? What musicians?" he asked excitedly.

The maid laughed. "Ah now, young sir, I cannot tell you that. I'm just a servant, and I know only what I hear." She paused and then added: "I can tell you one name I have heard mentioned—a Mr. Purcell, or something like that."

"*Purcell!*" Sullivan almost shouted. "Why, Father's band often plays his music. I can play some of it."

The thought that Henry Purcell, who, though born in the seventeenth century, was still considered England's greatest composer, had received his first musical training at the Chapel Royal fired Sullivan's imagination. Having himself an excellent voice, he implored his father to allow him to leave school to become a chorister. As was to be expected, Mr. Sullivan at first showed great reluctance, but eventually he sought the advice of an eminent musician, who expressed the opinion that, in view of the boy's enthusiasm and exceptional talent for music, it would be wrong to oppose his wishes.

So one day in the early spring of 1854, shortly before his twelfth birthday, Arthur Sullivan was taken by his headmaster, Mr. Plees, for an interview with Mr. Helmore at the Chapel Royal school in Cheyne Walk, Chelsea. On reaching Cheyne Walk, they found they had mistaken the address: the house where they thought Mr. Helmore lived was uninhabited and boarded at the windows. Mr. Plees snapped that he could not waste time looking for the right house, but Arthur, not to be thwarted, ducked into a butcher's shop and asked for the correct address.

Mr. Helmore, a fatherly but strict man, received them with great cordiality, and tested Sullivan's voice by giving him a song to sing to his own piano accompaniment. Without a hint of nervousness, Sullivan played the opening chords and broke into song in a rich treble voice, crystal clear on the highest notes. Mr. Helmore looked up at the ceiling in silent appreciation. The boy's voice is outstanding—far better than any other in the choir, he thought. He had no hesitation in accepting him as a chorister.

Sullivan's joy was inexpressible when, a few weeks later, he became a boarder at the choir school and was given his smart uniform of scarlet and gold tunic with knee breeches.

The Chapel Royal choir consisted of organist, choirmaster, eight men, and ten boys, know as "Children," who, in addition to their musical training, received a modest general education without cost to their parents. Their main duty was to sing in the chapel of St. James's Palace twice on Sundays, on saints' days, and on other special occasions such as royal marriages, births and funerals.

Every Sunday the choristers had to walk all the way from Chelsea to St. James's Palace, and back again, for the morning service, and then to repeat the journey for evensong. As they paraded through the streets, homeless, half-starved urchins would jeer in envy at their colorful uniforms and pelt them with stones. One Sunday soon after Sullivan joined the choir, the choristers were attacked by a party of ruffians near Buckingham Palace. Though they put up a stout defense, they were no match for their assailants. Luckily a man came to their rescue, and they escaped with only a few bruises and scratches.

This long trek to and from St. James's Palace so exhausted Sullivan that he would often return from the morning service in a state of collapse, and would spend the afternoon on his bed to recover his strength for the evening service. Fortunately, his delicate constitution did not interfere with his singing. When he had been a chorister for only a few months, he was selected as one of the soloists to sing at the opening of the Crystal Palace. Queen Victoria and the Prince Consort, who presided at the opening ceremonies, so admired his voice that they asked him to sing the solo parts of a new anthem at the christening of their next child.

For this high honor, Sullivan was trained by the composer himself, Michael Costa, an Italian with a curious pronunciation of English. Though he approved of Sullivan's singing, Costa did not think that the boy pronounced his words with sufficient clarity, and kept interrupting the rehearsals to demonstrate what he considered a better pronunciation. "Noo, noo, Soolivan," he would say. Then, throwing back his shoulders, he would sing the lines himself—"Soofer leetle cheeldren to kom onto me, and forbeed them not, for of sooch is the Keengdom of Hevan."

Suppressing his giggles, Sullivan would then try again. But, though he did his best to copy Costa's pronunciation at the rehearsals, he found this such a handicap to his singing that he pronounced the words in the correct manner at the actual ceremony. The Queen and the Prince were enchanted, and afterward they sent for Sullivan to congratulate him on his performance. The Queen asked him whether he wanted to make music his career.

"Oh yes, your Majesty, I do—more than anything!" Sullivan told her.

The Queen smiled graciously. "Then I hope that one day, Arthur, you will be a great musician," she said.

The Prince, who was a patron of the arts, dipped his hand into his pocket and presented the boy with a golden half-sovereign. "And here is a little reward to encourage you," he added with his strong German accent.

Sullivan goggled. "Oh thank you, sir. Thank you very much indeed. I have never had so much money before," he told the Prince.

The other choristers could not help but feel a little envious of the way Sullivan was making his mark, but he soon won their friendship by his modesty, winning manner, and bubbling sense of fun. Though he did not possess Gilbert's sparkling wit, Sullivan nevertheless could be just as gay. He decided to introduce a little gaiety into their leisure hours by forming the choristers into an orchestra.

"But we have only a piano! We can't form an orchestra with just a piano," the choristers objected.

"Oh yes, we can," Sullivan chuckled. "We can reproduce the other instruments by stretching paper over our combs and using them as mouth organs."

The other boys laughed. "But that's a child's game! You can't make music—not real music—with combs and paper!"

"Yes, yes, you can," Sullivan insisted. "It's only a knack. Listen to this!" He held the comb and paper to his mouth and blew a hymn tune as a violin might play it. He then repeated the tune in representation of several other instruments.

The choristers were amazed, but they soon acquired the knack under Sullivan's tutoring. In the evenings, and on their Saturday half-holidays when rain prevented their going out, they would gather around the piano to make music with their combs and paper in the same joyful spirit as Gilbert dined and joked with his theatrical cronies. Sometimes Sullivan's elder brother, Frederick, who had come to London to train as an architect, would join the party and add his talent by representing the cello, an instrument which he now occasionally played in a real orchestra.

Armed with a ruler as his baton, Arthur Sullivan would conduct a few old favorites to get the "orchestra" in full swing, and then change places with the pianist and improvise tunes of his own in the form of hymnal renderings of popular ballads. "Now, boys, hum me a tune," he would call out, his hands poised above the keyboard.

One of the choristers would start to hum a song then being sung by professional singers in the Victorian drawing rooms, and whistled by errand boys and murdered by barrel organs in the streets. After the first few strains, Sullivan would exclaim, "That's enough!" and, without pause for reflection, proceed to play the same tune in the style of a fugue such as a composer of sacred music might have written. As his hands moved reverently along the keyboard, the choristers would raise their combs and, after a few unmelodious splutters, take up the tune.

Sullivan's love of improvising led to his dabbling with compositions of a more original nature. He made a habit of composing madrigals in bed at night by the light of a flickering candle, quaking lest Mr. Helmore should walk into his dormitory and discover him at this. He then became more ambitious and composed a sacred song, which he bashfully showed to the organist of the Chapel Royal. The organist thought so highly of his composition that he promptly arranged for it to be sung by the choir at a special performance at Fulham Palace, as a result of which Sullivan was rewarded with another welcome half-sovereign by a future Bishop of London, who told him: "You are a clever boy. Perhaps one day you will write an oratorio."

Arthur Sullivan was coming to be regarded as the Chapel Royal's most gifted chorister since Purcell, and, at the age of fourteen, he scored a great triumph by becoming the first boy to win the Mendelssohn scholarship for the best young composer or performer of the year. This scholarship, established in memory of the great German composer, entitled Sullivan to two years' musical education at the Royal Academy of Music, in London, followed by a period of study in the German school of music at the Conservatory at Leipzig.

His parents, overjoyed at his splendid achievement, now finally agreed that Sullivan should make music his career. They still had grave misgivings about the hardships he might have to face but they now hoped and believed that his exceptional talents might eventually carry him to the top of his profession and make his struggles worthwhile.

For the next two years, Sullivan spent part of his day at the Royal Academy of Music, while continuing as a chorister at the Chapel Royal. At the Academy, where he also won immediate popularity, he studied many kinds of music under the best tutors of the day, and everyone, tutors and students alike, expressed amazement at his prowess and versatility. One student later wrote of him: "Sullivan's mastery of the orchestral instruments was incredible. He could play them all with absolute ease. Indeed, his ability in every department of music was stupendous. He could read anything at sight, play from the most formidable score, and clearly distinguish all combinations of sounds without seeing notes struck. Moreover, he seemed to grasp each new line of study in five minutes, where the rest of us took five months."

At the Chapel Royal, during this same period, Sullivan became leader of the choir, with the responsibility of supervising the special Saturday morning practices for the Sunday services. Mr. Helmore held such a high opinion of Sullivan's personal integrity that he gave him greater authority than he had ever accorded a leader before.

"I leave everything in your hands," he told him. "I shall always expect the highest standards, and I rely on you to see that these are achieved. Once you are satisfied with the singing, you may end the practice and all go out and enjoy yourselves."

Since the average Victorian master ruled with the rod, Mr. Helmore's broad-mindedness in relying upon Sullivan's sense of honor in this way touched Sullivan deeply. "I always recall my old master with affection and respect," he said many years later. So anxious was he not to betray the trust placed in him that he would sometimes keep the choir practicing well into the afternoon, thereby shortening their half-holiday; and, under his leadership, their standard was always of the highest.

Everyone at the Chapel Royal and the Academy was sorry when Sullivan's training ended and the time arrived for him to go to Leipzig. Mr. Helmore presented him with the Queen's bounty of £60 ($300) and a Bible for his services as a chorister and expressed the opinion that one day he would become a famous musician.

Sullivan smiled bashfully and replied in all sincerity: "If ever I do become famous, sir, I shall owe my success to you."

CHAPTER FOUR

Sullivan Studies in Germany

In 1858, when Sullivan entered the Conservatory, Leipzig was a romantic town of splendid Gothic architecture, with an ancient university and a rich tradition in music and art. Johann Sebastian Bach, as cantor of St. Thomas's church and school, had spent the last twenty-seven years of his life, from 1723 to 1750, and composed many of his greatest works at Leipzig. Now, more than a hundred years since his death, Leipzig was famed throughout Europe for its choral and orchestral concerts, operas, and, not least, for its Conservatory.

The Conservatory was founded by Felix Mendelssohn—who conducted the popular Leipzig Gewandhaus concerts—in 1843, four years before the composer's death. Though the academy was only fifteen years old when Sullivan became a student, it was already considered one of the best in the world.

Sullivan was captivated by the romance and tradition, but he soon found that very much higher standards were expected of him in Germany, the land of music, than in England. "I am obliged to work tremendously hard here," he wrote to his father shortly after his arrival. "No sooner is one master dispatched than I rush home to prepare for another." He was also severely handicapped by the fact that his tutors taught in German, a language he could not speak. "I do not understand a word they say," he observed despondently.

It was obvious that his only hope of really profiting from his scholarship was to learn German immediately and with the utmost speed. In desperation, Sullivan went to see the director of the Conservatory's pianoforte department, Ignaz Moscheles, who, having spent twenty years in London, was fluent in English. "Please, Mr. Moscheles," he appealed, "will you help me?"

Moscheles, who had known Beethoven and taught Mendelssohn, misunderstood his request and volunteered to give Sullivan some extra piano lessons in English, which solved only part of his problem, since most of his lessons would still be in German. "I was wondering," Sullivan said a little hesitantly, "if you could also teach me the language."

Moscheles raised his eyebrows in surprise. "Teach you German! H'm! . . . Do you know any German at all?" he asked.

"I have managed to learn a few words and a little grammar," Sullivan told him.

Moscheles grunted.

"I am sure I could soon pick it up with someone to help me," Sullivan pressed him.

Moscheles shrugged as though he doubted this, but agreed to give him what assistance he could. "Very well, very well, I will do my best to help you," he promised.

Sullivan studied German in every spare moment, so great was his sense of urgency and his determination to make the most of his scholarship. He took oral lessons with Moscheles whenever his master could spare him the time, and he spent most evenings in his shabby lodgings teaching himself grammar and vocabulary from textbooks. As his father had to pay for his keep, he would huddle in his overcoat to save the expense of a fire. As it was now winter, he often became numb with the cold, but, though tears might run down his cheeks, he would pore over his books until he was no longer capable of grasping their meaning.

After a month or two, Sullivan's dogged determination began to bring reward. Each week he found that he could understand a little more of his music lessons than the week before, until eventually, after some six months, he became sufficiently fluent in German to understand his masters completely. Once he had learned the language, he began to streak ahead.

"That is good—very good! You improve well. Every week you grow better!" one of his masters congratulated him in German when Sullivan went to him for a lesson in fugue at the house where Bach had lived.

Sullivan beamed. *"Danke schön, Mein Herr!"* he thanked him, airing his own German.

This was the first time he had been to this historic house, and he glanced around the room, with its fine oak-paneled walls and massive ceiling beams, marveling at the thought that it had once been Bach's home. "And Bach really composed here!" he sighed in awed reverence.

His master nodded. "In this very room."

Now that he was progressing so well, Sullivan, instead of shivering in his miserable lodgings, spent most of his leisure time going out and about with the other students, among whom were the Norwegian pianist and composer, Edvard Grieg, and the German-born operatic composer, Carl Rosa, who later was to establish the Carl Rosa Opera Company in England.

An English student, John Barnett, had an aunt living in Leipzig, and one evening he took Sullivan, Grieg and Carl Rosa to her house for supper. After supper, the four students, all of whom with the exception of Barnett were to become world famous, gathered around the piano and entertained their hostess and her two attractive young daughters, Clara and Rosamund, with an informal concert. Sullivan, whose voice had now broken, sang tenor and Carl Rosa bass, while Grieg and Barnett took turns with the piano accompaniment.

"That was delightful. Now you must all come again," Mrs. Barnett invited them when the time came to say good night. "You will come again, won't you?" she pressed Sullivan, shaking him warmly by the hand. She was enchanted by his ingratiating manner, and her daughter Clara had quite lost her heart to him. "He excites in me a strange emotion such as I have never felt before!" she confided to her sister after he had left the house.

Sullivan took advantage of Mrs. Barnett's invitation by spending nearly every evening at her home during the next few weeks. He began to return Clara's affection, but he really preferred her sister, who did not love him; and being only seventeen, he soon found the gay night life of Leipzig a greater attraction than either girl.

But much as he enjoyed this frivolity, it could not compare with the pleasure and satisfaction he drew from the concerts, especially those at the magnificent Gewandhaus, or Cloth Hall, where the cream of musicians performed. After one such concert, Sullivan hung about in the hall until nearly everyone had left, and had the thrill of meeting the famous Hungarian pianist and composer, Franz Liszt, who was then nearly fifty and the idol of the German musical world. Liszt, who was fond of a game of cards, invited Sullivan to make up a four at whist, and afterward accompanied him part of the way back to his lodgings. "Liszt was most amiable," Sullivan told his parents. "And what a wonderful player he is! He plays with such power, and yet with such delicacy and lightness. I would give the world to play the piano as Liszt does."

During his first year at Leipzig, Sullivan's ambition was

to become a great pianist, and he made such excellent progress that he was chosen to play at several concerts. But gradually the German education broadened his approach to music and sharpened his creative instinct. Like Liszt, Mendelssohn, and so many famous musicians who began as pianists, he developed a still greater ambition to be a successful composer. He therefore specialized in composition during his second year at Leipzig.

He began by composing an overture which, to his great delight, was performed at a Conservatory concert under his own baton. This was the first time he had conducted in public, and his masters were impressed by his skill and poise, as well as by his music. "Did you feel nervous?" one of them asked him afterward.

Sullivan seemed surprised at this question. "Nervous? Oh no, sir—not at all!" he assured the master. "It was great fun standing up and conducting that large orchestra."

He was to have the excitement of conducting several more of his compositions during the next few months, and on each occasion he was warmly congratulated upon the high quality of his composition and his handling of the orchestra.

The German tutors thought so highly of Sullivan's attainments as a composer, conductor and pianist that, when his scholarship period was drawing to an end, Moscheles urged him to remain at the Conservatory for an extra six months as a fee-paying student. "A little more study here may help you to rise to great heights," he told him.

Sullivan, thinking of the expense this would mean for his poor father, felt bewildered.

"I am sure you will never regret it," Moscheles pressed him, not realizing the reason for his hesitation. As

Sullivan still appeared hesitant, Moscheles invited him to think over his suggestion.

Sullivan spent the next week or so in an agony of mind debating whether to jeopardize his prospects by going against Moscheles' advice, or to ask his father to meet the fees for further study. Finally, he wrote to his father, who, at great sacrifice, sent him some of his savings. "My boy," he replied, "of course you must stay on."

Sullivan was at a loss for words to express his gratitude. "How can I thank you sufficiently, my dearest Father, for giving me this splendid opportunity?" he wrote. "I am indeed very grateful, and will work extra hard to show you that your sacrifices have not been in vain. And I will try to make the end of your days happy and comfortable."

When Sullivan went to tell Moscheles of his decision to remain at the Conservatory, he had a pleasant surprise. After expressing his pleasure at Sullivan's decision Moscheles said: "I am told that your father cannot really afford these fees, and therefore we have decided to keep you on without payment."

Sullivan gaped. "You mean . . ."

"Yes," Moscheles interrupted him, beaming genially, "you have proved such an outstanding pupil in every way that we are prepared to make an exception for you by waiving your fees."

Sullivan was overcome with emotion and could only stutter his thanks.

His six months' extra study was to benefit him in a way that not even Moscheles could have foreseen. One day while he and some friends were out for a walk, Leipzig was suddenly hit by the worst storm in its history. Black clouds turned day into night, a raging gale swept the town, and then, like the rattle of machine-gun fire, hailstones described as being the size of hens' eggs pelted down.

Chimney pots crashed to the ground, tiles were torn from the roofs, and every window facing west in the town was shattered. Many people were injured, and cattle in the fields killed, but Sullivan and his friends took shelter under an old archway. This must surely be the end of the world! they thought as they huddled together, too scared to speak.

When the storm subsided, Sullivan waded through the flooded streets back to his lodgings, only to find the building under water and temporarily uninhabitable.

The storm, which lasted for less than ten minutes, created such a deep impression on Sullivan that it inspired him to set Shakespeare's play, *The Tempest,* to music—a composition that was shortly to spring him to sudden fame.

In April 1861, shortly before his nineteenth birthday —the age at which Gilbert became a Privy Council clerk— Arthur Sullivan left the Conservatory and returned to London to earn his living. He could not adequately express his gratitude to his German masters for all they had taught him. "I often try to think," he said, "what might have become of me had I never come to Germany."

CHAPTER FIVE

Sullivan Makes His Name

Arthur Sullivan began his musical career as organist at a fashionable church in Pimlico, whose choir consisted almost entirely of women. Strongly disapproving of this, he surprised the vicar by marching straight to the nearest police station to recruit some male voices from the local police force.

These policemen could sing reasonably well by ear, but were unable to read music or to differentiate between the various notes. At their first practice Sullivan struck a chord and asked them to name the key, but the policemen, as erect as on parade, remained as silent as the church statues. "Come, come, now don't all speak at once!" Sullivan teased.

At this, one policeman, feeling that somebody ought to say something, called out the first letter to enter his head: "B, sir." To his embarrassment, Sullivan then fired the question: "B major or B minor?"

Having never heard of either, the policeman took another chance and replied smartly: "B minor, sir."

Sullivan, bubbling with mirth, called his bluff, and everyone laughed. In spite of this unpromising start, the policemen soon began to respond to Sullivan's painstaking instruction, with the result that in the course of a few months he built up one of the best church choirs in London.

Meanwhile, Sullivan had the good fortune to meet George Grove, the secretary of the Crystal Palace. Impressed by Sullivan's charm and by his reputation as a student, Grove appointed him Professor of Pianoforte and Ballad Singing at this important musical center; and this post, though involving very little work and not at all lucrative, indirectly started him on the road to fame.

At that time British appreciation of music was limited almost exclusively to the compositions of Mendelssohn and Handel, and only the works of the greatest composers were performed at the Crystal Palace. However, in April 1862, a year after Sullivan's return from Leipzig, Grove took the bold step of including Sullivan's music to *The Tempest* in the program—and most unexpectedly, the audience went into raptures.

After the performance, Charles Dickens, like many others, rushed backstage to congratulate Sullivan. "I don't pretend to know much about music," he said, gripping him firmly by the hand, "but I do know I have been listening to a very great work." Though Dickens was then fifty and Sullivan not quite twenty, their meeting was soon to blossom into a close friendship.

The critics were equally enthusiastic. One musical magazine described Sullivan as "the perfect master of his art," while two or three others paid him the highest compliment by linking his name with Mendelssohn.

So generous was the acclaim that a repeat performance of *The Tempest* was given at the Crystal Palace a few days later, when, a newspaper reporter tells us, "all the beauty and chivalry of London, lovely ladies in frills and bustles, and handsome gentlemen in frock coats and top hats, flocked to Sydenham in their smart carriages to hear Sullivan's music."

Like Gilbert with his first play, *Dulcamara*, Sullivan made a name for himself overnight, but was still a long way from lasting fame and fortune. Indeed, he earned so little that he was barely able to support himself, and sometimes had to go short on food to pay his rent, although his lodgings were the cheapest he could find.

"Don't lose heart, my boy!" his father encouraged him when once he appeared a little depressed. "Why, you have met already with more success by the age of twenty than most musicians achieve in a lifetime! Persevere, and eventually you will reach the top."

Young Sullivan smiled and said resolutely, "Yes, Father, I must and will succeed. But if only," he sighed, "I could compose a real masterpiece!"

His father took his hand. "Patience, my boy! Inspiration of real genius is rare, but one day it will come to you. Meanwhile, you must be content to undertake any work that may come your way."

Arthur Sullivan bore his hardships in his usual cheerful spirit, and worked harder than ever. He obtained a second post as organist, coached pupils at his shabby lodgings in the evenings and gave part-time instruction at the Chapel Royal, where his old master also did all in his power to encourage him.

In the hope of meeting influential people who might help to build up his reputation, Sullivan also joined one of the choral societies which then used to sing at the large private dinner parties of London's leading hostesses. In this way, he met Mr. Gladstone. On two occasions when the choral society sang at his home in Carlton House Terrace, the Liberal leader joined in the singing and elected to stand next to Sullivan to share his score; and on the second occasion, he led him afterward into a corner of the room to discuss the technicalities of music. "Now perhaps you will kindly explain to me the process of musical composition," Mr. Gladstone invited Sullivan.

Sullivan stroked his mutton-chop side whiskers, which he had recently grown, wondering how to condense so broad a subject into a few words. "Well, now, let me see," he began. Before he could say any more, Gladstone pompously cleared his throat and proceeded to answer his own question—quite inaccurately.

A little later, at another dinner party, Sullivan met Benjamin Disraeli, the Tory leader, who asked him the same question. Disraeli, on the contrary, listened attentively to Sullivan's explanation and had the grace to thank him. "Well, it is still a wonder to me," he said, flipping a piece of fluff from his colorful waistcoat, "but you have made many things much clearer."

Like his sovereign, Queen Victoria, Sullivan liked Disraeli better than Gladstone.

Busy as he was, Sullivan also found time to compose a number of ballads of a kind then popular in the drawing rooms, selling the copyright of each for only £5 ($25). Several of his songs were inspired by a Crystal Palace director's attractive daughter, with whom he had fallen madly in love.

Soon after Sullivan's twenty-first birthday, the couple became secretly engaged, deciding not to tell their parents until they could afford to marry. When, as so often happens, their secret leaked out, the girl's parents were furious; and the girl, rather than face their anger, meekly broke off their engagement. "Our hopes," she said, "can never be fulfilled. All is over."

Sullivan was heartbroken. Indeed, it has been suggested that it was because of this unhappy experience that he never married.

Repeated performances of *The Tempest* in London and the provinces, and the growing popularity of his songs, for which he received so little, gradually enhanced Sullivan's reputation and thereby eased his struggles, until finally, at the age of twenty-four, he was given his opportunity to compose his "masterpiece." He was invited to compose one of the main items for an important music festival to be held at Norwich in the autumn of 1866.

"My whole future depends upon this one work," Sullivan told himself—and this thought caused him such deep anxiety that he immediately felt all at sea. He struggled to find a good and original theme, but he could get no inspiration. Day after day, he would get out his pen and ink and music paper to toy with an idea, only to discard it after composing a page or two; and at night he would toss and turn in bed, his mind in a whirl. The harder he drove himself, the more impossible his task became.

After weeks of anguish, Sullivan, worn out by worry and loss of sleep, finally unburdened himself to his father. "Father," he said, "I am in despair! This commission means so much to me, but now I fear I shall have to turn it down."

His father exclaimed in horror, "No, no, my boy, you must not do that! Do not give up on any account! You still have several weeks in which to compose your piece, and something is sure to occur to put new vigor and thought into you."

Sullivan heeded his advice and waited, and in the end his father himself gave him his inspiration—but in a way that caused him the greatest grief.

At four o'clock one morning, Frederick called at his lodgings and awoke him with the news that their father had been taken seriously ill. Arthur Sullivan sprang out of bed and threw on his clothes; and the two brothers jogged in a hansom cab through the ill-lit streets, with their flickering gas lamps, to their parents' home. There they learned that their father was dead. Arthur Sullivan broke down and wept piteously: "My dear, dear father whom I loved so passionately! Oh, it is so hard—so terribly hard—to think that I shall never see his dear face again, or hear his cheery voice . . ."

So great was his grief that he became like a ghost, his face deathly pale, his brilliant eyes lifeless, and his brain dulled. For a week, he could not set his mind to anything —but then he felt a sudden urge to pour out his sorrow in music, and composed *In Memoriam.*

This, his last tribute to his father, was the inspiration he had been seeking. *In Memoriam* was performed at the Norwich Festival in October, and its immediate popularity finally brought Arthur Sullivan into the front rank among composers—in just the same way as Gilbert's play, *The Princess,* finally established him as a playwright.

Sullivan, though naturally relieved and gratified, was extremely modest in the face of success. A true artist, his one desire now was to develop British appreciation of music beyond just Mendelssohn and Handel by introducing the works of some of the great composers then unknown in England. Few people in England knew Schubert and Schumann even by name, but in Germany they had an immense following. Sullivan, who had come to share the Germans' love and admiration of both these composers while studying at Leipzig, persuaded Grove to include occasionally one of their compositions in the Crystal Palace concerts. Encouraged by their reception, he decided to carry his crusade a stage further. Some of the music of Schubert, who had died in Vienna in 1828, had been lost since his death, and Sullivan resolved to bring these manuscripts to light.

This seemed a vain hope to Grove, but he readily agreed to accompany Sullivan on a visit to Germany and Austria in search of them. First, they visited Schumann's widow, at Baden, to see if she could throw any light on the subject; but Frau Schumann could tell them nothing. After making further fruitless inquiries, they eventually went to Vienna, where they called on a music publisher named Spina. Spina had no information either, but he led them to a room piled high with dusty manuscripts, and invited them to search through these, hospitably producing a box of cigars to help them over their labors.

Sullivan and Grove spent a week wading through this unwieldy mass, but found nothing. As they were scrabbling through the last pile, Spina's clerk—a dear old man with a skull cap who had often served Beethoven in the shop—limped into the room and suggested their visiting a Dr. Schneider, who was related to Schubert. "The doctor has several cupboards full of manuscripts," the old man told them. "You might find something there."

Dr. Schneider, whom they visited the following day, presented them with more great stacks of musical scores. But again they were unlucky. They were on the point of abandoning their hunt and returning home, when Dr. Schneider mentioned casually that he had it in his mind that he had once possessed the manuscript of Schubert's *Rosamunde.*

"*Rosamunde!*" Sullivan almost shouted. "Why, that is one of the works we're looking for!"

"Are you sure you have not still got it?" Grove pressed the doctor.

Dr. Schneider scratched his head. "I can't think where it could be," he replied, and then added as an afterthought: "There is one cupboard I have not been through, but I feel sure there is nothing of interest in there."

Grove eagerly took him up on this. "Would you mind if I were to have a look? . . . After all, there's always a chance!"

Dr. Schneider shrugged. "By all means look if you wish. But I warn you: you'll get smothered with dust! The place has not been tidied out for years!"

Like a dog ferreting out a rabbit, Grove nosed his way into the cupboard and rummaged through its contents. Some five minutes later, begrimed and spluttering, he emerged triumphantly with the entire score of *Rosamunde*. A further search brought to light the original manuscripts of a Schubert overture and two of his symphonies.

The two men sat up until two o'clock in the morning copying out the parts, ending their labors by leapfrogging joyfully around the room. Next day, they started home for England with their precious discoveries, breaking their journey at Leipzig, where Sullivan conducted his *In Memoriam* and received rapturous applause.

During the early years of his career, Sullivan composed only serious music, a great deal of which, perhaps on account of his training at the Chapel Royal, was of a sacred nature. It was the editor of *Punch,* F. C. Burnand, who first persuaded him to break into the field of light opera. He and Sullivan were both members of a music and literary society that used to meet once a week at a private house at Campden Hill, in London, for an evening's discussion and entertainment. After a light supper, at which vast quantities of oysters would be consumed, a short play might be staged, or perhaps a comic opera by Offenbach, the composer of *The Tales of Hoffmann.*

One evening, while walking home together after watching an Offenbach opera, Burnand told Sullivan that he had just written a burlesque to raise money for the widow of a member of his staff. "I was wondering if you would compose the music for it?" he added inquiringly.

"Me!" exclaimed Sullivan. "But I have never written that sort of music before!"

After some persuasion, Sullivan agreed to try his hand at composing something in the style of Offenbach, whose operas, though popular, had not the same appeal in England as in Germany. He took so long to get his heart into this that he did not complete the music for Burnand's burlesque, *Cox and Box*, until a few hours before its first performance, and he managed that only by working all night with the aid of two copyists, who grabbed and copied the various parts as each was finished. However, his efforts were crowned with success. After an initial performance in a private house, *Cox and Box* was produced at the Adelphi Theatre, where it was highly acclaimed, and ran for three hundred nights.

Snatches of Sullivan's new light music began to be hummed and whistled, just as Gilbert's light verse was quoted and parodied. The way was now paved for their partnership.

CHAPTER SIX

Gilbert and Sullivan Go
into Partnership

Gilbert and Sullivan met at an entertainment gallery in London's Lower Regent Street in the autumn of 1869. Gilbert was thirty-two, a tall, military figure, with mustache and side whiskers, fair hair receding from a broad forehead, and a fresh, ruddy complexion. Sullivan was twenty-seven, short, plump and sallow, but dapper in his dress and personal appearance, and also imposing. They were as different in character as in looks.

Gilbert's loveless and unsettled childhood had made him autocratic and independent, and consequently very temperamental. When he was pleased with life, he would be courteous and charming; but he was apt to lose his patience upon the smallest pretext, directing his biting wit against the person who had gained his displeasure, and perhaps following this up with legal action. Naturally, this thoughtless disregard of other people's feelings made Gilbert many enemies. On the other hand, his powerful personality and brilliant sense of humor outweighed his shortcomings and won him far more friends and admirers. His personality was, indeed, so forceful that even those with whom he quarreled most bitterly could not help but feel a certain respect for him.

Sullivan, having been brought up under very much happier conditions, in spite of his parents' poverty, had a tender loving nature, and would never say or do anything to hurt anyone. Unlike Gilbert, who did not care a rap what anybody thought of him, Sullivan deliberately courted popularity by going out of his way to be pleasant in whatever company he might be. No one could help liking Sullivan. Even so, most people in the theatrical profession had a higher regard for Gilbert, difficult as he was, on account of his stronger personality.

Two men so different in their ways and outlook could not be expected to form a close friendship, but their sparkling sense of humor and ability to give expression to it in their respective arts gave Gilbert and Sullivan a priceless bond for a business relationship. Since each preferred and considered himself better at serious work than at comic opera, neither Gilbert nor Sullivan felt any inclination to collaborate. But they could not escape their destiny.

They were introduced at the entertainment gallery by Fred Clay, who had set several of Gilbert's burlesques to music. Gilbert happened to be in the course of writing a blank-verse play, one of whose characters was a musical pedant. Possessing not the smallest knowledge of music, Gilbert had consulted an encyclopedia for the meaning of the word "harmony" and translated the definition into verse without understanding a word of it. Fearing that what he had written might be pure nonsense, he took advantage of his introduction to Sullivan to obtain the reaction of a professional musician.

"Ah, Sullivan, I am glad of this opportunity of meeting you—very glad indeed!" Gilbert breezed. Without further formality, he then posed his conundrum. "Now perhaps you will be kind enough to give me your opinion. I maintain that if a composer . . ." He launched into a stream of high-sounding musical technicalities. "Well, what do you say? Does that make sense?" he inquired on finishing his monologue.

It was so clever that Sullivan was floored. "Well," he said after Gilbert had recited the rigmarole a second time, "you have certainly raised a most interesting point, but I fear I cannot give you an answer offhand. I must have time to think it over."

This conundrum—to which Sullivan never gave Gilbert an answer!—forged the first link between the two men. A few months after their meeting, they were persuaded, rather against their will, to collaborate in a comic opera, which they called *Thespis*.

Thespis was a Greek actor of the sixth century B.C. who introduced various stage innovations into the ancient Dionysian festivals of that country, and who is now generally regarded as the father of Greek tragedy. Gilbert hit upon the idea of making the weary gods of Mount Olympus change places with Thespis and his troupe of actors for a period of one year. One amusing high light of this transformation is that Bacchus, the god of wine, gives place to a teetotaller, who causes the grapes to yield only ginger beer.

Gilbert, being the librettist, attended to the casting and stage production, while Sullivan looked after the musical side. In musical productions of that time the chorus would be engaged simply to sing, and would parade on the stage like a platoon of soldiers, taking no part in the acting. Gilbert, who by now had learned a great deal about stage management from his friend Tom Robertson, considered this practice ridiculous. "I refuse to have my chorus looking like a lot of stupid dummies!" he snorted. "They must act—give life to the show!"

Since very few singers were capable of acting, Gilbert reversed the usual procedure by choosing his chorus for their acting ability rather than for their voices. Naturally, this imposed a severe restriction on Sullivan, who protested: "How do you expect me to compose music for actors and actresses who cannot sing?"

"How do you expect *me*," Gilbert retorted, "to produce an opera with singers who cannot act?"

At this, they both laughed. "All right, have it your own way!" Sullivan chuckled. "I will compose the music to suit your chorus, but it will not be easy as none of them can compass more than six notes!"

When rehearsals started, Gilbert was quickly forced to the conclusion that his cast possessed no great gift for acting either. The principal artists were awkward in their movements, rather like puppets on strings, and they spoke and sang their lines in an absurdly unnatural way, exaggerating the dramatic passages by overraising their voices and gesticulating. This style of performance was to be expected in the cheap music halls, but it did not pass muster with Gilbert. "No, no—that won't do at all!" he snapped. "Now you go and stand over there!" he ordered one of the leading ladies, pointing to an unobtrusive part of the stage.

The actress, who had been giving herself airs and graces, resented being ordered about in this manner. "Really, Mr. Gilbert," she sulked, "why should I stand here? I am not a chorus girl!"

"No, madam," Gilbert flashed with customary wit, "your voice is not strong enough, or no doubt you would be!"

After so gross an insult, it would not have been surprising if she and the rest of the cast had walked out, but they decided that it was better to face Gilbert than to lose their jobs. Gradually, by constant badgering, Gilbert trained his cast to get life into their performance. Instead of posing and declaiming, and treating each song as an individual turn, they began to throw themselves into their parts with real feeling, threading their items together into a complete story, like the chapters of a book. The result was scintillating and nobody felt happier than the players themselves.

Thespis opened at the Gaiety Theatre on Boxing Day, 1871, and Sullivan, who conducted the music, afterward congratulated Gilbert upon his production. "I have never seen anything so beautiful on the stage before," he said.

Gilbert returned the compliment by congratulating Sullivan upon his music, but Sullivan considered this undeserved. "No, no, the music went badly," he replied in all sincerity. "One of the principal singers sang half a tone sharp throughout! It was dreadful!"

Gilbert, being tone-deaf, had not noticed this, but apparently the music did not appeal to the audience either, for the scores were never published, and *Thespis,* though highly praised as a stage production, ran for only a month.

Deciding that there was no future for them in light opera, Gilbert and Sullivan went their separate ways and spent the next four years or so writing and composing independently again.

Gilbert returned to his true love of writing straight plays, some in prose and others in blank verse, which flowed from his pen in a steady stream that seemed unlikely ever to run dry. Like so many Victorian plays that have failed to survive, they were overloaded with sentiment and showed no outstanding literary merit, but Gilbert and his critics thought them wonderful, and they earned him a great deal of money.

He could afford to join an expensive club, to own a yacht, and to ride with the well-to-do in Hyde Park's Rotten Row. But he did not spend his money only upon himself. At his home in fashionable South Kensington, a large house requiring several servants, he began to give splendid parties for the children of his friends and neighbors.

Gilbert, who still hoped to have children of his own, would fool and romp with his small guests like the best of fathers—a lovable side of his character in marked contrast with the martinet the actors and actresses knew.

Sullivan, meanwhile, devoted himself to composing songs and sacred music. Two of his most notable compositions of this time were the hymn *Onward, Christian Soldiers* and a *Te Deum,* to celebrate the recovery of the Prince of Wales (later Edward VII) from a severe attack of typhoid fever.

Queen Victoria, who by now had been widowed for more than ten years, had not forgotten the day when Sullivan sang so exquisitely at the christening of her child, and she seemed to take a personal pride in his success as a composer. Besides commissioning him to compose music for special occasions such as this, the Queen, and indeed, the royal family generally, began to treat Sullivan as a friend. Her second son, the Duke of Edinburgh, having inherited his father's interest in the arts, felt especially drawn toward Sullivan and started inviting him to his house parties at his country home at Ashford, in Kent.

In view of his rather humble background, Sullivan might well have felt out of his depth in a royal household and have shown himself to a disadvantage, but, on the contrary, he was at perfect ease and behaved like a polished courtier, paying careful attention to etiquette and generally acting with grace and tact. During the course of dinner on his first visit, Sullivan overheard someone say that the Duchess played the piano well; and so, when later the gentlemen joined the ladies in the drawing room, he bowed politely to his hostess and tactfully requested her to play for the company.

The Duchess, though touched by this charming little courtesy, graciously declined. "You are very kind, Mr. Sullivan," she smiled, "but I could not play in front of so distinguished a musician as yourself . . . Perhaps *you* will play for us?" she invited him.

Sullivan bowed and suggested: "If you do not wish to play solo, perhaps your Royal Highness will do me the honor of accompanying me in a duet?" Before she could answer, he held out his hand and led the Duchess to the piano.

They played several duets by Schubert, and everyone was enchanted. Sullivan warmly complimented the Duchess as they rose from their piano stools—and this was not idle flattery. Thereafter, they made a practice of playing together in the evenings whenever Sullivan stayed with the Duke and Duchess.

In 1873, a new music center was founded to allow young people of talent to be trained for a musical career regardless of their parents' income or social position. This school, which has since become the Royal College of Music, had originally been suggested by the Duke of Edinburgh's father, the Prince Consort; and the Duke, who became its first president, offered Sullivan the post of principal.

Sullivan at first refused to consider the appointment as he was afraid that the school might become a rival to the Royal Academy of Music, where he had received the first part of his Mendelssohn scholarship training. "I owe so much to the Academy," he explained, "that it would not be right to associate myself with a rival."

"There is no danger of rivalry," the Duke assured him, and renewed his appeal. "You are the obvious choice . . . I beg of you to accept."

Eventually, Sullivan yielded to pressure and became the principal, but he did not settle happily to his task. Though he did an excellent job in setting the college on its feet, he so disliked organizing and teaching that he resigned when the center had become firmly established.

Meanwhile, in 1875, when Sullivan had been the principal for some two years, he and Gilbert were unexpectedly thrown together again as the result of a chance meeting in the street between Gilbert and the manager of the Royalty Theatre in Soho, Richard D'Oyly Carte.

D'Oyly Carte, a bouncing little man of thirty-one with a pointed beard and heavy mustache, was warmhearted, of striking personality, and so extremely astute that he was known in the theatrical profession as "Oily Carte." His genius lay in spotting and promoting talent where other theatrical managers might have been unwilling to risk their money. D'Oyly Carte firmly believed that a partnership between Gilbert and Sullivan, in spite of the discouraging reception of *Thespis,* offered immense possibilities; and his unexpected meeting with Gilbert now jolted him into making a proposition on the spot. "Ah, Gilbert, you're just the man I want to see," he said heartily. "I have been thinking about you and Sullivan—you should get together again!"

Gilbert ridiculed the idea. "Oh no, no, there's no sense in that! We have had one try, and it did not work out. We don't want a second failure."

"But, my dear fellow," exclaimed D'Oyly Carte, "you must not base everything upon one show! A second opera might prove a brilliant success."

Gilbert grunted.

"Seldom have two men had so much to offer each other," D'Oyly Carte went on. "A partnership between you and Sullivan might easily earn you both a fortune!"

"Well, well, I'll think about it," Gilbert promised impatiently in the hope of ending the conversation.

But D'Oyly Carte would not be satisfied with an empty promise. "Good," he breezed, "then you had better start thinking now, for I have an offer to make. I would like you and Sullivan to collaborate in writing me a one-act piece as a curtain raiser to an Offenbach opera which I intend to produce shortly . . . Now, will you agree to this, if Sullivan is willing?" he urged Gilbert.

Gilbert did not feel that he could be bothered to write a special piece, but it happened that he had recently dramatized a magazine sketch which he thought might possibly suit the purpose. So he mentioned this to D'Oyly Carte. "It is a skit on the British legal system, based on my own unfortunate experiences at the bar. The story is centered on a case concerning a breach of promise of marriage, and I thought of calling it *Trial by Jury*," he said, adding, "Of course, it's very trivial. But it might fill the bill."

D'Oyly Carte read and liked the sketch, and eventually persuaded Gilbert and Sullivan to meet and discuss the project. Accordingly, one snowy morning in the depth of winter, Gilbert, with a great deal of grumbling and grunting, put on his heavy fur overcoat, stuffed the script of *Trial by Jury* into his pocket, and slithered off through the icy streets to see Sullivan.

Seated by a roaring fire, Gilbert, whose humor was not improved by the weather, read his script aloud to Sullivan like a sulky schoolboy resentful of an imposition. After the first two or three pages, he broke off and growled: "This is really very stupid—a waste of time reading it!" Sullivan, who was chuckling to himself, motioned Gilbert to continue before he lost the thread. With mounting indignation, as though he considered the sketch beneath his dignity, Gilbert read to the end and then closed the manuscript with an impatient snap.

Sullivan now let himself go and laughed uproariously. Gilbert stared. "You mean to say you like it?" he asked incredulously.

"Like it!" Sullivan spluttered. "My dear chap, I think it's superb! It's the wittiest libretto I have heard in years! We can really do something with this."

They accepted D'Oyly Carte's offer without further hesitation, and got down to work. Sullivan felt so inspired that he composed the music for *Trial by Jury* in under three weeks; and Gilbert, roused by his enthusiasm, attended to the production and casting in the same buoyant spirit.

To achieve reality, Gilbert arranged for the scenery to be an exact reproduction of the Clerkenwell Court House, where he used to appear as a young lawyer with such dismal results. He paid the same careful attention to the choice of his artists. Refusing to be influenced by their professional standing, he took immense pains to find actors and actresses really suited to the parts, causing a certain amount of resentment by giving the important part of the Judge to Sullivan's brother Frederick, who, being an architect by profession, was naturally only an amateur actor. As was to be expected, the professional artists felt slighted, and accused Gilbert of favoritism; but his choice was admirably justified. Frederick had a natural talent for acting, which Gilbert had been quick to detect, and he played the Judge with great distinction.

Trial by Jury was produced at the Royalty Theatre in Soho on March 25, 1875—only a month after Gilbert and D'Oyly Carte had met on the street—and it created a sensation. Gilbert and Sullivan, the critics agreed, had set a new standard in light opera. "So perfect is the accord between liberettist and composer," wrote one musical expert, "that, as in the great operas by Wagner, poem and music seem to proceed simultaneously from one and the same brain." So great was its popularity, indeed, that, instead of being merely a curtain raiser, *Trial by Jury* soon took the place of the Offenbach opera as the main item. D'Oyly Carte's prophecy that a second Gilbert and Sullivan opera might prove a brilliant success had come true.

There could be no more argument now about their

future: Gilbert and Sullivan agreed to go into partnership in a new light-opera company to be formed by
D'Oyly Carte—a partnership that was to last for almost a
quarter of a century.

CHAPTER SEVEN

Triumph

Before he could form his company, which he decided to call the Comedy Opera Company, Richard D'Oyly Carte, not having sufficient capital of his own, had first to persuade a few people with money to support him, and this did not prove at all easy. The financiers whom he first approached considered his venture far too risky. They thought the popularity of *Trial by Jury* was a one-time phenomenon, and that Gilbert and Sullivan were unlikely to repeat their success with another and longer opera. "Audiences often get excited over something new, but they will soon grow tired of this sort of nonsense!" they scoffed. One and all declared: "There's no money to be made in comic opera."

Eventually, D'Oyly Carte managed to obtain financial assistance from some music publishers, and took a lease on a rambling old theater known as the Opera Comique, situated below ground in a maze of narrow streets and alleys. The Opera Comique adjoined another theater, The Globe, and the dividing wall between them was so thin that the muffled voices of the actors and actresses in The Globe could often be heard as a background to the performances in the Opera Comique.

The theaters were approached by a long tunnel, and

theatergoers not on the alert were liable to lose their way and enter the wrong auditorium. The Prince of Wales once went to see a comedy at the Opera Comique but instead saw a tragedy at The Globe. The performers themselves, when arriving with only a few minutes to spare before their act, would sometimes, in their haste, dart through the wrong stage door, a very easy mistake for an actor who, at various times in his career, might have acted at both theaters.

D'Oyly Carte's choice of the Opera Comique did not meet with Gilbert's approval. "This won't do!" he sniffed on going to inspect the place. But it had to do, for there was no better theater available, and certainly no money to build a new one.

Besides grumbling about the theater, Gilbert also bickered with D'Oyly Carte over the terms of their contract —a subject from which Sullivan, being easygoing, preferred to hold aloof. After arguing for several weeks with only partial success, Gilbert, a little ruffled, settled down to writing a two-act opera, *The Sorcerer,* based on another of his magazine stories. He intended to give the principal male lead to Sullivan's brother Frederick, who had made such a hit in *Trial by Jury,* but before *The Sorcerer* was finished a tragedy occurred: Frederick was suddenly taken ill and died.

Arthur Sullivan was distraught. He seldom left his brother's room throughout his illness; night and day, he sat at his bedside, comforting Frederick and trying to console himself by reading poetry. One day he read a verse by a minor poet, Adelaide Procter, that exactly expressed his feeling of misery and helplessness at that moment:

> Seated one day at the organ
> I was weary and ill at ease,
> And my fingers wandered idly
> Over the noisy keys.

Shortly after Frederick's death, Arthur Sullivan set these words to music under the title of *The Lost Chord*—a song that was to become one of the most popular of the age.

As after the death of his father, when he had been inspired to write *In Memoriam,* so now Sullivan felt as if his whole world had collapsed. He could not bring himself to go anywhere or to meet anyone for fear of breaking down. The only people he would see were his mother and Frederick's young widow and children, for whose welfare he now felt responsible, and to whom henceforth he always showed the greatest kindness and generosity.

Sullivan's grief was made even more unbearable by his own poor health for, though only thirty-four, he had recently developed a severe kidney complaint that was beginning to undermine his constitution. This disease, which was to prove incurable and gradually grow worse, caused Sullivan spasms of such acute pain that sometimes he would collapse in the middle of what he was doing and slump practically unconscious. Normally, he bore his complaint with great fortitude, never allowing it to affect his good humor, but now, in his unhappy frame of mind, it reduced him almost to the breaking point.

For many weeks after his brother's death, Sullivan shut himself away in his London apartment—where he now lived in comfort with a manservant to look after him—and just brooded. Gilbert mailed him the manuscript of *The Sorcerer* and urged him, as tactfully as he could, to make a start at composing the music; but Sullivan felt too ill and dispirited even to attempt this. Gilbert, though nearly frantic, showed the gentler side of his character by coaxing Sullivan into action with friendly notes of encouragement; and Sullivan finally responded by settling himself down at his table and driving himself to compose. Though this required a supreme effort, the cloud of depression began to lift once he had made a start, and he soon became absorbed in his task.

The Sorcerer followed the ever popular theme of love, and had not the freshness and sparkle of *Trial by Jury*, but Gilbert made the very most of the opera by the high quality of his production. Once more he showed great daring by refusing to engage any professional actors and actresses of experience, and relying instead entirely upon beginners and amateurs. He was sick of artists who, having made their name, thought they knew everything. Temperamental tenors, who threatened to walk out on the slightest provocation, were his special bugbear. "They never can act, and are more trouble than they are worth!" he snapped when informing Sullivan of his decision.

Sullivan, who never interfered with Gilbert's production arrangements, could not help wondering whether his partner was taking too great a gamble in dispensing with all the professionals. "You don't think you are being a little drastic, that it might be wise to employ them for the principal parts?" he queried a little hesitantly.

But Gilbert would not hear of this. "No, no, definitely not. We must make a clean sweep!" He would have no one with fixed ideas and irritating stage affectations; he wanted a cast of enthusiastic young men and girls whom he could train from the beginning and order about, like a master sergeant drilling recruits for the army.

Gilbert searched for likely talent, and, with the same brilliant perception he had shown in selecting Frederick Sullivan for the Judge in *Trial by Jury*, unearthed two completely unknown young men, George Grossmith and Rutland Barrington, for the two leading male parts. Barrington had done a little acting in minor theatricals, but Grossmith was a drawing-room entertainer with no experience of the stage. It is doubtful if anyone but Gilbert would have given them an audition. Not surprisingly,

D'Oyly Carte's company directors took fright. "They are horrified at your choice!" D'Oyly Carte told Gilbert.

"I don't care a hoot if they are! Tell them to mind their own business!" Gilbert retorted.

D'Oyly Carte, who had complete confidence in Gilbert's stage management, laughed. "I know how you feel," he humored him, "but the trouble is that this *is* their business! Don't forget they are partly financing the show! They are afraid of losing their money!"

"Money! Money!" Gilbert scoffed.

"We can't do without it!" D'Oyly Carte chuckled, and went off to placate his fellow directors.

No one was more surprised at Gilbert's choice than Barrington and Grossmith themselves, both of whom felt most unsuited to their parts.

"I should have thought," remarked Grossmith with a puzzled frown, "that, with so much singing, you would require an actor with a good voice, a far better voice than mine."

"No, no, that is just what I do *not* want," Gilbert assured him.

Barrington was curious to know what had prompted Gilbert to cast him as a parson. "That's quite simple," Gilbert replied airily. "You said that your father once wanted to be a clergyman, did you not? Very well, then you must have the church in your blood!"

The choice of Barrington was perhaps the more surprising because his part involved a great deal of singing, and yet he had very little ear for music. "Why *did* you choose him?" Sullivan, foreseeing more difficulties for himself, pressed Gilbert.

His reply was typical: "Because he seems the staid, stolid type I want."

In fact, Gilbert simply had a hunch that Grossmith and Barrington had a natural talent for comic opera, and, as in the case of Frederick Sullivan, his hunch proved correct. The two men were of quite different temperament, Grossmith being high-strung and Barrington extremely placid, but Gilbert knew how to bring out the best in each of them; and they were to become two of the most popular stars of the company.

Some forty to fifty beginners and amateurs took part in *The Sorcerer,* and, though Sullivan had an uphill struggle to teach many of them to sing, he too worked wonders. All excelled at the opening performance, which took place at the Opera Comique on November 17, 1877.

The opera received generous acclaim and ran for six months. The enthusiasm of the theatergoers, however, was patchy, with the result that the box-office receipts soon began to fluctuate, sending D'Oyly Carte's fellow directors into a perpetual dither. "The audience is falling off! Take the show off before we lose money," they would order D'Oyly Carte. With his usual astuteness, D'Oyly Carte would persuade them to hold on for another month. The receipts would then go up again and everybody would be happy, until the next drop. And so it went on. D'Oyly Carte, as well as Gilbert and Sullivan, grew heartily sick of the directors, but they could not carry on without them —not yet.

While the directors were seesawing between enthusiasm and despair over *The Sorcerer,* Gilbert skimmed through his *Bab Ballads* and newspaper clippings of recent events for an idea with a topical twist to work up into another opera. His clippings reminded him that the well-known news agent and bookseller, W. H. Smith, who had begun life as a newsboy, had recently been appointed First Lord of the Admiralty without having had any experience of the sea. In view of Britain's long tradition as a great sea power, this appointment struck Gilbert as faintly ridiculous, and so he decided to poke gentle fun at British politics and the navy by writing a skit of life on board ship—the good ship *H.M.S. Pinafore.*

With boyish enthusiasm, Gilbert outlined the plan of his latest little bit of topsy-turvydom to D'Oyly Carte, who was greatly tickled. He could not discuss the idea with Sullivan as he had just gone to Paris on the invitation of the French government to supervise the music at an important exhibition—an honor for which he was afterward decorated. However, Gilbert sent him the gist of the story by letter, commenting: "I feel sure you will be pleased. There is so much scope for fun!"

Drawing upon six or seven of his *Babs Ballads,* Gilbert concocted a hodgepodge of delicious nonsense, one of whose principal characters, Sir Jospeh Porter, K.C.B., has risen to the post of First Lord of the Admiralty from office boy in a firm of lawyers, his origin being twisted to avoid offending W. H. Smith.

Accompanied by "his sisters, and his cousins, and his aunts," the First Lord rides out to sea and boards *H.M.S. Pinafore,* proudly proclaiming in song:

> I am the monarch of the sea,
> The ruler of the Queen's Navee,
> Whose praise great Britain loudly chants.

Whereupon his relations break in to introduce themselves:

> And we are his sisters, and his cousins,
>   and his aunts!

The First Lord rollicks on:

> When at anchor here I ride,
> My bosom swells with pride,
> And I snap my fingers at a foeman's taunts;

As also—". . . do his sisters, and his cousins, and his aunts!"

> But when the breezes blow,
> I generally go below,
> And seek the seclusion that a cabin grants!

And, of course—". . . so do his sisters, and his cousins,
                              and his aunts!"

Having touched upon his nautical habits, the First Lord musters the officers and crew and a party of girls assembled on deck, and describes his rise to his exalted position in another rollicking song:

> When I was a lad I served a term
> As office boy to an Attorney's firm.
> I cleaned the windows and I swept the floor,
> And I polished up the handle of the big front door.
> I polish'd up that handle so carefullee
> That now I am the ruler of the Queen's Navee . . .

> As office boy I made such a mark
> That they gave me the post of a junior clerk.
> I served the writs with a smile so bland,
> And I copied all the letters in a big round hand—
> I copied all the letters in a hand so free,
> *And* now I am the ruler of the Queen's Navee . . .

> In serving writs I made such a name
> That an articled clerk I soon became;
> I wore clean collars and a bran-new suit
> For the pass examination at the Institute.
> And that pass examination did so well for me,
> That now I am the ruler of the Queen's Navee . . .

> Of legal knowledge I acquired such a grip
> That they took me into the partnership,
> And that junior partnership I ween,

Was the only ship that I ever had seen.
But that kind of ship so suited me,
That now I am the ruler of the Queen's Navee . . .

I grew so rich, that I was sent
By a pocket borough into Parliament;
I always voted at my party's call;
And I never thought of thinking for myself at all.
I thought so little, they rewarded me,
By making me the ruler of the Queen's Navee . . .

The First Lord then gives a word of advice as to how others might follow his example—

Now landsmen all, whoever you may be,
If you want to rise to the top of the tree,
If your soul isn't fettered to an office stool,
Be careful to be guided by this golden rule:
Stick close to your desks and never go to sea,
And you all may be rulers of the Queen's Navee!

The purpose of the First Lord's visit to the *Pinafore* is to woo "the gallant captain's daughter," Josephine, but she, alas, has lost her heart to an able seaman, Ralph Rackstraw, with whom she plans to elope. When the First Lord, on hearing of this, tries to forestall them by ordering Ralph to be put in chains, Little Buttercup, a bumboat woman who has come aboard to sell groceries, makes the startling announcement that many years ago, when Ralph Rackstraw and the ship's captain, Captain Corcoran, were babies, she had taken them both into her home and had subsequently switched their identities: Rackstraw, though serving as a seaman, was in fact of good birth, whereas the meticulously correct Captain Corcoran, who prided himself on never swearing whatever the emergency—"I never use a big, big D"—was really of very humble parentage. After this amazing reve-

lation, the Captain and the seaman change places; and the
First Lord, unable to bring himself to marry the daughter
of a common sailor despite his professed pride in his own
humble beginnings, leaves Josephine to her Ralph.

H.M.S. Pinafore, one of the wittiest and most scintillating of his *librettos,* took Gilbert only a few weeks to write.
Sullivan, on his return from Paris, expressed great delight. "My dear Gilbert, you have excelled yourself!" he
chuckled, turning the pages of the manuscript to re-read
the First Lord's song. "Yes, yes," he muttered, mentally
setting a tune to the song, "I like it enormously. You
have got such a nice easy swing into the whole opera . . .
I only hope my music will do it justice!"

Sullivan began the musical composition immediately,
but, though he was bubbling with inspiration, his painful
kidney complaint repeatedly ground him to a halt. "I
would compose a few bars and then lie almost insensible
with pain," he later told a friend. "When the paroxysm
was passed I would write a little more, until the pain over-
whelmed me again." On several occasions, his valet
found him huddled on his couch practically unconscious,
and tried to send for the doctor, but Sullivan always refused to hear of this. "No, no, there's nothing the doctor
can do," he would gasp. "Leave me alone, and I shall be
all right shortly."

It was surprising that Sullivan was capable of composing in these conditions, but, in spite of all his distressing
interruptions, he managed to maintain continuity and
to inject an infectious gaiety into his music that perfectly
matched Gilbert's libretto.

Gilbert was delighted. "Now the next thing is to go
down to Portsmouth," he said after congratulating Sullivan on his score.

"To Portsmouth! Whatever for?" Sullivan asked.

Gilbert winked and drew erect. "To inspect *H.M.S.*

Pinafore, of course! If you look at the manuscript, you'll see that she's lying off Portsmouth harbor!" He laughed. "We must produce this show properly or not at all! My object in visiting Portsmouth is to inspect some of the ships in harbor to help me visualize the scenery and general atmosphere. Will you come with me?"

"Why, certainly, of course I will," Sullivan agreed. "But surely," he added dubiously, "it will be necessary to get Admiralty permission. Isn't it rather a nerve to ask for this? I mean, well, we are not being very polite to the navy!"

"It is all arranged. I have already approached the Admiralty, and been promised the necessary facilities," Gilbert announced with an air of achievement.

A few days later, the two partners went to Portsmouth, where they were taken in an Admiralty launch on a tour of inspection. After boarding and examining three or four ships anchored in the channel, they returned to the harbor to inspect Nelson's flagship, *Victory,* in which the great Admiral lost his life at the Battle of Trafalgar. Gilbert made detailed sketches of the *Victory*'s quarter-deck, while Sullivan chatted to a naval officer and jotted down some general notes.

On their return from Portsmouth, Gilbert, having now a vivid mental picture of the scenery and general effect for which to aim, got out his drawing pad and set to work constructing on paper the quarter-deck of his imaginary *H.M.S. Pinafore,* based on the information he had gleaned.

Before the carpenters built the set, Gilbert ordered them to make him a small-scale model of the scenery and to cut him a number of chunks of wood with flat bases, some of three inches and some of two and-a-half inches, to represent the actors and actresses. With the aid of these models, Gilbert now spent several hours each day systematically going through the script of *H.M.S. Pinafore* and working out the movements of the performers, scene by scene. Like a chess player, he would hesitantly advance one little chip, representing perhaps George Grossmith, to a certain position on the stage, but might then detect a more subtle move and take it back again. So anxious was he to achieve perfection, that he worked out every item of the production in the minutest detail before starting rehearsals.

The first rehearsals were not encouraging, but Gilbert himself was to blame for this: he had broken his new rule by engaging a professional actor of quite long standing and an actress who had frequently sung in Italian opera; and both artists proved extremely truculent. The actor seemed incapable of following a perfectly simple stage direction, and when Gilbert finally raised his voice at him, he took deep exception and angrily shouted back: "No, sir, I object! I have been on the stage quite long enough."

"Quite!" Gilbert flashed—and forthwith dismissed him from the cast.

The actress took offense because Gilbert would not allow her the central position on the stage every time she appeared. "But this is where I stand in Italian opera!" she objected.

"Unfortunately, madam, this is not Italian opera, but only a low burlesque!" Gilbert snubbed her. Then she also left the cast.

There was no more serious trouble after their departure. Even so, several little incidents occurred to try Gilbert's patience. George Grossmith, for instance, once unwisely tried to score himself an extra laugh by deliberately tripping and rolling on the floor. The rest of the cast thought this very funny, but Gilbert considered that it cheapened the turn, and reprimanded Grossmith: "Kindly omit that!"

Grossmith was crestfallen. "Certainly, Mr. Gilbert," he replied timidly, but he then made matters worse by going on to express the opinion: "I should get a good laugh from it."

"So you would if you were to sit on a pork pie!" Gilbert jibed.

Rutland Barrington also caused minor consternation by destroying part of the scenery. "Sit on the skylight over the saloon—*pensively*," Gilbert ordered him. Unfortunately, the skylight was not strong enough to bear Barrington's weight, and he fell through. Since this was a genuine accident, and no one was hurt, Gilbert joined in the merriment and chuckled: "That's *expensively*—not pensively!"

Barrington's little mishap seemed very trivial by comparison with the trouble he was causing Sullivan by his poor ear for music. During the first few weeks, he murdered every song in his repertoire, until it really began to look as if he might have to be replaced by another actor. Sullivan, though at times in despair, kept his sense of humor and treated his shortcomings as a joke. "That's a very good tune indeed, but now let's have mine!" he would tease after Barrington had croaked a succession of wrong notes. Another actor sang so badly that Sullivan threw up his hands and laughingly exclaimed: "In future, I had better get you to sing my songs first, and then compose them afterward!" He made similar remarks to most of the cast at various times, but he never harried anyone; and his superb patience and sympathetic understanding brought him rich reward.

The behavior of Gilbert and Sullivan at rehearsals, as might be expected, contrasted strongly. Sullivan was consistently kind and gentle, but Gilbert was not so predictable. At the early rehearsals, before the members of the cast were familiar with their parts, Gilbert gave them the kindliest encouragement, praising those who were quick to learn, and showing endless patience with others who were slower, and never displaying the least trace of irritation or temper except when disobeyed or deliberately thwarted. By this soft, methodical spade work, he gradually brought their latent talents to the surface—and was rewarded by discovering that he now had a promising young actress, Jessie Bond, to coach to stardom.

Having won the confidence of the cast and installed them in their parts, Gilbert became far less tolerant. At the start of every scene, he would give them a stern reminder of the importance of getting vigor into their performance by bawling from the stalls: "You have got to give your all in this passage, or it will fall flat!" If they failed to do their best, he would roar them to a halt and break into a tirade of unseemly language. "Gilbert is the only man I have ever met who can swear straight on for five minutes without stopping to think and without repeating himself!" one of the cast observed. Having thus expressed his feelings, Gilbert would bound on to the stage and proceed to prance around, coat tails flying, demonstrating the correct way to play the parts. The actors and actresses had the greatest difficulty in suppressing their giggles on these occasions, and when once an actor failed to control his mirth Gilbert turned in fury and knocked him down.

One moment Gilbert would be a lamb, the next a lion —according to how a rehearsal was going. He often kept the performers rehearsing until as late as three o'clock in the morning, driving them nearly crazy with his fussiness for detail and turbulent outbursts, but, however bad-tempered he had been, he always ended on a gentle note. Switching from the lion to the lamb, he would thank them for all their hard work, express satisfaction at their progress, and send them home by taxi at his own expense.

The cast, though in awe of Gilbert, melted at these little gestures, respected his high standards, and braced themselves for the next day's rehearsals. By a mixture of gentle coaxing and extreme irritability, Gilbert molded the cast of *H.M.S. Pinafore* into a brilliant team; and after the final dress rehearsal, he praised them generously. "If the play succeeds," he told them, "the credit will be yours, but, if it fails, the fault will be ours."

On the evening of the first performance, on May 25, 1878, Gilbert was in a state of high tension lest anything should go wrong. He darted in and out of the dressing rooms to make sure that everyone was happy and ship-shape, and then darted onto the stage to satisfy himself that the scenery was in order. Finally, a few minutes before the curtain was due to go up, the strain proved too much for him, and he astonished Sullivan, who was perfectly calm—which was just as well since he had to conduct the orchestra!—by announcing: "I can stand this no longer! I'm going for a walk!"

Grabbing his hat and stick, Gilbert rushed out of the theater, and wandered aimlessly up and down the streets of London throughout the performance. Returning just as the last act was finishing, he listened anxiously outside the stage door for the audience's reaction. The music stopped . . . a moment's pause . . . and then—a storm of applause. Gilbert gave a loud sigh of relief, and, like a puppy let out of its kennel, bounded onto the stage to join Sullivan for the curtain call.

"Everything went magnificently, Gilbert, *magnificently!*" Sullivan told him excitedly after they had acknowledged the applause perhaps half a dozen times. "Listen to them, they're still calling for us!"

H.M.S. Pinafore was indeed a dazzling success, and it offended nobody. W. H. Smith, who made a good First Lord of the Admiralty, took the joke well; while a high-ranking officer from the Admiralty who went to see the show a few nights after the opening wrote to congratulate Gilbert and Sullivan: "I was perfectly delighted with *Pinafore*. It is quite excellent."

The popularity of the opera increased with every performance. "My dear, have you seen *Pinafore?*" people began to ask each other. "No? Then, go at once! It's the best show in years!"

Before very long, Americans were also going "mad about *Pinafore*"—but this, far from pleasing Gilbert, Sullivan and D'Oyly Carte, made them furious.

CHAPTER EIGHT

The Partners Go to the United States

The reason for their anger was that American theatrical producers were pirating the Gilbert and Sullivan operas. There was at this time no copyright agreement between Britain and the United States to protect the rights of British and American authors and composers. And there was nothing to prevent an American promoter from producing *H.M.S. Pinafore* without the permission of Gilbert, Sullivan and D'Oyly Carte, and, what was worst of all, without paying any fees or royalties for these performances.

As a result, when *H.M.S. Pinafore* became a hit in London, theatrical and concert managers in many parts of the United States took the opportunity to stage their own garbled versions of the opera, and the partners had no legal power to restrain them.

"The position is preposterous!" Gilbert exploded. "I refuse to write another libretto if the Americans are immediately going to steal it! . . . We must do something immediately to put a stop to this! If we cannot go to law we must act in some other way."

All three men were resolute in refusing to submit to this injustice, but they agreed that, before deciding upon their line of action, D'Oyly Carte should first go to the United States to explore the situation.

On his arrival in New York, D'Oyly Carte discovered that *H.M.S. Pinafore* was playing to packed houses nightly in no less than eight theaters in that city alone, at six others in Philadelphia, and at some thirty to forty playhouses in towns and cities throughout the United States. Some people, he discovered, had been to the opera a dozen times or more. Extracts from *Pinafore* were even played and sung in churches. A Boston church choir once sandwiched a selection of *Pinafore* songs between parts from a Mass by Mozart and Handel's "Hallelujah" chorus.

While organs thundered Sullivan's music in churches, thousands of barrel organs churned it out in the streets. The songs rang through the length and breadth of the United States, their popularity far surpassing those of any previous light opera. Clearly, a great many people were making a fortune from the work of Gilbert and Sullivan.

D'Oyly Carte went to see performances of *Pinafore* at some of the New York theaters, and he was appalled at the poor quality of the productions. The scenery and stage effects seemed amateurish by comparison with Gilbert's. The singers ruined the libretto by introducing labored gags that interrupted the rhythm and tempo, and destroyed the subtlety of Gilbert's humor; and the orchestras failed to catch the spirit of Sullivan's music. The productions were so bad that D'Oyly Carte drew courage.

He sent Gilbert and Sullivan a full report of his investigations, and urged them to follow him to the United States immediately, and to bring with them some of the artists from the Opera Comique with a view to staging their own production in New York with a combined British and American cast. Displaying once again his astuteness and foresight, D'Oyly Carte confidently predicted:

"If we can show the Americans how *Pinafore* should really be played, we shall defeat the pirates. I am sure the Americans will appreciate the difference between our production and these slapdash versions. Then we shall have the field to ourselves."

"He's right!" Gilbert said when he read D'Oyly Carte's report. "We'll go to America immediately and fight these unscrupulous agents on their own ground!"

Sullivan agreed. "It's the only thing to do!"

Gilbert stumped along to the Opera Comique to select the artists to play the leading parts and then feverishly set to work polishing up the understudies who were to replace them while they were away. Sullivan then took over and repeated the laborious business of transforming amateurs with indifferent voices into accomplished singers.

A few days before they were to sail, Sullivan's kidney trouble flared up and he had to undergo an emergency operation. The operation, though not a cure, was as successful as could be expected; and, after a delay of nearly a month, Gilbert and Sullivan sailed for America with their small party of actors and actresses, reaching New York in November 1879.

News of their visit had apparently spread throughout the city, for they received a joyous welcome. As their ship approached the harbor, a number of small steamers, decorated with Union Jacks and the Stars and Stripes, chugged out to greet them with bands playing tunes from *Pinafore*. And when Gilbert and Sullivan landed, newspaper reporters swarmed around them, buzzing with questions. With great difficulty, D'Oyly Carte eventually extricated them and conducted them to the house where they were to stay, but the reporters were on their heels.

During the next few days, the reporters called at the house at all hours, requesting interviews. Sullivan, feeling still far from well, found this a great strain; while Gilbert often felt intensely irritated by this intrusion, that delayed their work. However, they hid their feelings, and answered the numerous questions with patience and courtesy. Assuming an air of false modesty, they expressed astonishment at the fuss being made over them—and the reporters thought them wonderful. They sharpened their pencils and wrote at length about the charm and genius of the two Englishmen who were "honoring" America by their visit, a line of publicity to which Gilbert and Sullivan raised no objection!

Gilbert hurriedly scouted around at the New York theatrical agencies in search of suitable American actors and actresses for the chorus and minor parts, and then coached and rehearsed them with the same mixture of gentleness and firmness as he had employed at the Opera Comique. Meanwhile, Sullivan trained them to sing and enlisted an orchestra.

The American performers showed no fear of Gilbert and responded quickly to his coaching, fitting in admirably with the British actors and actresses who were to play the major parts. The feathers began to fly, however, at the first dress rehearsal, when Gilbert's critical eye found fault with some of the costumes. "They need shortening. Please see that this is done in time for tomorrow morning's rehearsal," he asked the wardrobe master.

"By tomorrow morning! But that's impossible! It can't be done," the harried young man replied.

Gilbert flushed. "Can't, sir? Did you say can't? . . . But my dear sir, it must be done!"

At this the wardrobe master lost his temper and his self-control and sprang at Gilbert, lashing at him with his fists. The cast ran to Gilbert's aid, and forcibly removed the young man. Gilbert then sent for the theater manager, who apologized profusely, and promised to see that the order was executed. "Certainly, Mr. Gilbert, the dresses will be ready by tomorrow morning. The dressmakers shall not go home until the job is finished, not even if they have to work all night."

In less than a month, the combined British and American cast, and also the orchestra, had reached the same high level of performance as the London company. It was a tremendous achievement on the part of Gilbert and Sullivan, and on December 1, they gave their first performance of *H.M.S. Pinafore* at the Fifth Avenue Theatre. Sullivan, dapperly dressed and perfectly possessed, conducted the orchestra, but Gilbert again gave way to his nerves by walking the streets and then returning for the curtain call.

The audience, the majority of whom had already seen the garbled versions and were familiar with the tunes, gave the partners a delirious ovation. As D'Oyly Carte had predicted, they could well appreciate the superiority of their production over the pirated travesties—and so could the music critics.

"Last evening," one newspaper commented the following morning, "*H.M.S. Pinafore* was under the command of its builders . . . It was studded with new points . . . When the scene opened, the sailors were all seen at work attending to various ship's duties, while the whole was under the supervision of the busy and important little Midshipmate. This gave an animation to the first scene which it generally lacks . . . But the really noticeable difference in the interpretation was the orchestration. There was breadth, color, tone, together with an harmonious blending with the vocalism which was utterly wanting in what may be called the 'home-made Pinafores' . . ."

Since there had been so many "home-made Pinafores," Gilbert and Sullivan were afraid that the enthusiasm for

their own version might soon wane. So they wisely decided
to cash in on their popularity immediately by giving New
York an opera that had not yet been produced in London:
The Pirates of Penzance, inspired by Gilbert's kidnaping
in Naples at the age of two. They planned the opening
performance for New Year's Eve, which gave them just
under a month in which to do everything.

Gilbert had written the libretto before leaving England,
but Sullivan had still to compose most of the music. The
scenery and costumes had to be designed and made, and
the cast had to learn and rehearse their new parts while
continuing to play *H.M.S. Pinafore* nightly. Their target
seemed impossible, but everyone co-operated magnificently, the artists putting in such long hours each day that
they were nearly dead with fatigue by the time they went
to bed.

Sullivan had a particularly arduous and difficult task.
Instead of being able to teach the singers and the
orchestra the score when the opera was finished, he had
to interrupt his work to teach them each song as soon as it
was ready, in order to give them time to become familiar
enough with the music to do it justice. Then he would go
on to compose the next song. After spending most of the
day composing or rehearsing *The Pirates of Penzance,* he
would conduct the orchestra at the evening performance
of *H.M.S. Pinafore,* and then sit up most of the night composing again.

He had such a race against time that he did not finish
the score until nearly six o'clock on the morning of New
Year's Eve—just about twelve hours before the opening
performance. He snatched a few hours' sleep, gobbled
down his breakfast, and hurried along to the theater to
rehearse the chorus and orchestra. He then collapsed from
the strain, and spent the afternoon in bed in acute pain
from his kidney complaint.

Gilbert was shocked at Sullivan's condition when he went into his room to see him. "You must not think of conducting the orchestra tonight. I will make other arrangements. Everything will be all right, so don't worry," he said tenderly.

Sullivan forced a smile. "No, no—I'll manage," he insisted. "It's just another spasm. It will soon pass."

"But, my dear chap, it would be madness for you to conduct! Stay in bed until you are really well," Gilbert implored him.

But Sullivan refused to give in. An hour or two later, wincing with pain, he staggered out of bed and dressed; struggled along to a restaurant, where he brought himself back to life with a glass of champagne and a dozen oysters; and then went on to the theater. When he strode in to take his place on the conductor's stand for the opening performance of *The Pirates of Penzance,* he managed somehow to appear as cheerful and dapper as ever.

He felt sincerely cheerful at the end of the performance. "I never saw such a beautiful combination of color and form on any stage. Some of the girls looked as if they had stepped out of a Gainsborough picture," he complimented Gilbert. He also felt rather pleased with his music, considering it superior to that of *H.M.S. Pinafore:* "tunier, more developed, and of a higher class altogether."

The audience found the opera captivating. They seemed to enjoy particularly the song by the police sergeant who went out with his force to catch the pirates—

> When a felon's not engaged in his employment . . .
> Or maturing his felonious little plans . . .
> His capacity for innocent enjoyment . . .
> Is just as great as any honest man's,
> Our feelings we with difficulty smother . . .

When constabulary duty's to be done.
Ah, take one consideration with another,
A policeman's lot is not a happy one . . .

When the enterprising burglar's not a-burgling . . .
When the cut-throat isn't occupied in crime . . .
He loves to hear the little brook a-gurgling,
And listen to the merry village chime . . .
When the coster's finished jumping on his mother . . .
He loves to lie a-basking in the sun.
Ah, take one consideration with another . . .
The policeman's lot is not a happy one . . .

The amusement of the audience reached its height when, as the policemen lay in wait, the pirates, armed with burglary tools, entered steathily, singing at the tops of their voices:

> With cat-like tread,
> Upon our prey we steal,
> In silence dread
> Our cautious way we feel!
> No sound at all,
> We never speak a word,
> A fly's foot-fall
> Would be distinctly heard . . .

The Pirates of Penzance created an even greater sensation in the United States than *H.M.S. Pinafore,* and its increased popularity was largely due to the fact that it was produced in the first place by Gilbert and Sullivan, and had not been distorted by others. Even so, attempts were soon made to "pirate *The Pirates.*"

Unscrupulous theatrical managers hired shorthand writers to sit in the auditorium and take down the words of the libretto, and out-of-work musicians to memorize and jot down the themes of the various tunes. They tried to bribe members of the orchestra to lend their scores for copying, and, when they were unsuccessful in this, they even stooped to theft. Small gangs of men would break into the theater at night to steal not only the music, but also the scenery and props. Gilbert, Sullivan and D'Oyly Carte managed to scotch them by posting guards in the theater to protect their property, but several hand-to-hand fights occurred before the thieves were driven off.

Realizing that attempts would be made to pirate the opera in other towns, Gilbert and Sullivan decided to foil them by hastily forming a number of repertory companies to send on tour with *Pirates of Penzance*. They set to work with feverish energy, sometimes rehearsing as many as four companies at the same time—a terrible strain for poor Sullivan who, though in almost constant pain, nevertheless refused to spare himself. In record time, these repertory companies were weaving their way to most of the principal towns of the United States, and the piratical managers never had a chance. Americans were not content with shoddy imitations when they could see the brilliant genuine production.

Having won the hearts of America, the partners returned to England in the spring of 1880 and produced *The Pirates of Penzance* at the Opera Comique, where it met with the same spectacular success.

CHAPTER NINE

Savoyards

The Gilbert and Sullivan operas were by now earning so much money that D'Oyly Carte could afford to buy out the company directors and become financially independent— a day to which they had all been looking forward.

D'Oyly Carte had made legal arrangements for this shortly before his trip to the United States, but during his absence the directors had committed an unpardonable act of treachery. Though in the first place they had agreed most willingly to sell their interests, the subsequent high box-office returns of *H.M.S. Pinafore* on both sides of the Atlantic had since made them regret their folly and driven them to do some pirating of their own.

While the three partners were in New York, the directors had sent a gang of ruffians to the Opera Comique with orders to break up a performance of *H.M.S. Pinafore* and forcibly seize the scenery and properties. They had hoped that this might intimidate the actors and actresses into deserting D'Oyly Carte and working for their own new rival company. The bewildered cast, far from submitting, had engaged the intruders in a fierce fight on the stage and driven them off. Their plot having failed, the directors, though possessing little or no theatrical knowledge, had finally mustered a cast of unemployed actors and actresses and presented their pirated version of the opera at a theater only a few doors away from the Opera Comique.

When, on his return from New York, D'Oyly Carte discovered this treachery, he was incensed. "I shall take legal proceedings against these people immediately," he said, and went off to put the matter into the hands of his lawyers.

While the lawyers were drawing up their case, Gilbert and Sullivan dealt their new rivals a bitter blow by their triumph with *The Pirates of Penzance*. People had been going to the pirated production of *H.M.S. Pinafore* simply to see how it compared with the authorized version, but, now that there was a new opera to be seen, they flocked back to the Opera Comique. Consequently, the box-office returns of the rival company quickly dwindled to practically nothing—and they never picked up. For, when the directors appeared in court to answer D'Oyly Carte's charge of infringement of copyright, they were sternly rebuked and ordered to close down.

D'Oyly Carte now resolved to fulfill a second great ambition: instead of renewing the lease of the Opera Comique, he decided to build his own theater—a decision that delighted both Gilbert and Sullivan.

"Splendid—splendid!" Gilbert kept repeating. "I never liked the Opera Comique. The stage is too cramped for comic opera."

"Yes, and the theater is no good for music, either," Sullivan put in. "The acoustics are very bad."

"We have been badly hampered all 'round," Gilbert went on.

D'Oyly Carte laughingly agreed that they had both worked miracles to achieve such splendid results under such difficult conditions, and promised to build them the best theater in London.

Together, they chose a site where the old Palace of Savoy, once occupied by John of Gaunt, had stood, and, in view of this historical association, they decided to call their new theater The Savoy. They took immense pains over the planning, providing for every convenience and comfort they could think of for both artists and audience, and commissioned one of the best architects in London to build the theater.

During its construction, Gilbert wrote *Patience,* an opera poking fun at the Aesthetic Movement, then sweeping London, to the delight of some and the disgust of others.

Leading figures in art and literature, revolting against the oppressiveness of Victorian art and taste generally, were trying to introduce "a new freedom and romanticism of literary and artistic expression" by drawing inspiration from styles and theories of much earlier periods. For example, the painter, Edward Burne-Jones, who designed stained-glass windows for churches, sought inspiration from the Italian Renaissance artists Botticelli and Fra Angelico; while his friend William Morris introduced a lighter and brighter style in household decoration, in particular in wallpapers. The doctrine of the Aesthetic Movement was "art for art's sake," and many famous artists followed this theme in all sincerity, and with a good measure of success; but the movement had been reduced to ridicule by the absurd behavior of the admirers of the dramatist Oscar Wilde, one of the principal aesthetes.

Oscar Wilde, supremely conscious of his brilliant wit, always liked to be the center of attraction. He used to focus attention upon himself by assuming poses that made him appear different from other people—by wearing clothes that did not quite conform to style, with an unusual flower in his buttonhole; by allowing his hair to

grow overlong; and by crowning other people's remarks
with witty repartee and generally dominating the conversation in whatever company he might be.

As an aesthete, Oscar Wilde affected to detect "art" in
the most commonplace things, making pretense that to
a man of his brilliant perception all life was flowery and
wonderful. Though his artistic appreciation undoubtedly
went deep, his behavior was so exaggerated that it was
surprising that anyone should take him seriously. However, thousands of young people began to imitate Oscar
Wilde. Young men posed as aesthetes by wearing plush
suits, by allowing their hair to fall over their ears and
down their necks and by adopting ridiculous mannerisms.
Intense young men and women searched for subtle mean-
ings that were never intended by their authors in books
and general literature, in paintings, and even in things of
nature. This was happening all over the British Isles.

Gilbert, who had met and taken a dislike to Wilde, was
critical of this "hot-house" trend, and decided to mimic
the dramatist in the character of a fleshy poet named
Reginald Bunthorne, with whom four languid aesthetic
maidens believe themselves to be in love, but who himself
has eyes only for Patience.

Bunthorne's song about the Aesthetic Movement might
have been written by Wilde himself, so well did Gilbert
capture his mood:

If you're anxious for to shine in the high aesthetic line as a
man of culture rare,
You must get up all the germs of the transcendental terms,
and plant them everywhere.
You must lie upon the daisies and discourse in novel phrases
of your complicated state of mind,
The meaning doesn't matter if it's only idle chatter of a
transcendental kind.
And every one will say,

As you walk your mystic way,
"If this young man expresses himself in terms too deep for
  me,
Why what a very singularly deep young man this deep young
  man must be!"

Patience, first performed at the Opera Comique in
April 1881, caused an immediate stir. People went in
such numbers to see the opera that every night the theater
was packed beyond capacity, and a great many theatergoers had to be turned away. However, when the show
had been running for some six months, D'Oyly Carte
was able to announce that his splendid new theater was
finished and that *Patience* was to be transferred to The
Savoy.

Tastefully decorated in white, pale yellow and gold—
a refreshing change from the heavy "gingerbread" style
then in vogue—The Savoy was a great improvement upon
the average Victorian theater. The audience and artists
alike were provided with comforts and luxuries they had
never experienced in a theater before. In the old Victorian theaters, many people in the audience found themselves tucked around corners or behind pillars that ob-
structed their view of the stage. The auditorium of The
Savoy was planned to allow everyone, including people
standing in the orchestra and balcony, to see the show
without craning their necks or standing on tiptoe.

The Savoy had another claim to distinction: it was the
first theater in Europe to be lit by electricity instead of
gas. A critic of *The Times* who inspected the building a
week before the opening reported with amazement:
"About 1,200 lights are used, and the power to gen-
erate a sufficient current for these is obtained from large
steam engines, giving about 120 horsepower, placed on
some open land near the theater."

Since this was the first attempt in London to light any

form of public building by electricity, the opening of The
Savoy Theatre, on October 10, 1881, caused exceptional
excitement, the unusually distinguished audience including the Prince of Wales, dukes and duchesses, foreign
diplomats, and many other people in high society. As
London's leading hosts and hostesses entered the bril-
liantly lit auditorium, they caught their breath in wonderment at its gaiety and dignity, so different from the
somber atmosphere of most other theaters.

Peeping from behind the scenes, Sullivan watched the
auditorium fill, and was captivated by the colorful evening dresses and glittering jewels of the ladies in the orchestra and yellow-draped boxes. "I have never seen such
a wonderful spectacle!" he said in a loud whisper, beck-
oning Gilbert to his peephole.

Gilbert, however, was too agitated to look: he was on
tenterhooks lest the electricity should fail, or some other
hitch occur to spoil the effect. A few minutes before the
curtain rose, he scuttled out of the theater to walk off his
nerves. This had become his regular practice, not only
on "first nights," but at every performance: not once
during the rest of his long partnership with Sullivan could
he be persuaded to watch one of their operas.

Even Sullivan, normally quite unaffected, felt a little
flutter on this occasion as he strode in to conduct the
orchestra. But everything went without a hitch. The elec-
tric lights gave an occasional disconcerting flicker, but the
old pumping engines on the wasteland outside managed
to keep them going, and the audience sat enraptured.
Their applause at the final curtain was deafening. Again
and again, they called for Gilbert and Sullivan, though
forgetting poor D'Oyly Carte, the builder of The Savoy.

The critics described the opening of The Savoy as the
start of a new era in theater management, and this was
no exaggeration. In nearly all theaters of that time there

was a great deal of laxity—largely due to their inefficient planning. This often caused discontent among the actors and actresses and made it difficult for them to work as a team. At the Opera Comique, Gilbert and Sullivan had encountered many inconveniences that were extremely damaging to discipline, and they had determined to overcome these problems and to leave no possible loophole or laxity or inefficiency at The Savoy.

Gilbert imposed many restrictions on the cast, and moreover, he introduced a scale of fines to ensure their obedience. In the future, the artists were to be fined for bad or indifferent work even at rehearsals—for muddling their lines, for example, or for introducing gimmicks of their own, as Grossmith was so fond of doing.

"This is like being back at school," the cast grumbled among themselves, but they soon got used to it.

They could not justifiably complain as Gilbert, Sullivan and D'Oyly Carte themselves set an example in self-discipline and teamwork. Though Gilbert was solely responsible for the libretto and Sullivan for the music, they worked in closest consultation in all matters concerning the actual production of an opera. Gilbert always obtained Sullivan's approval before finally deciding upon the scenery, costumes and other such matters, and, if Sullivan saw anything to criticize, they would try to reach a compromise. D'Oyly Carte had no say in the choice or production of an opera, but confined himself entirely to the business management of the theater, which he handled with great efficiency without interference from either the librettist or composer.

Gilbert and Sullivan also followed a routine in writing and composing their operas. First, Gilbert would draft the outline of his story, tearing it up and rewriting it perhaps a dozen times before it met with his satisfaction. Then he read this aloud to Sullivan to see what he thought of the musical possibilities. "Be frank, my dear fellow," he would invite his partner, "and say if there is any part you are not quite happy about." Occasionally, Sullivan might suggest a few alterations, but usually he saw little or nothing to criticize.

They would then analyze the story together to make sure that it would be within the understanding of the least intelligent section of the audience, a point which they both considered of the highest importance.

Satisfied about this, Gilbert would start work on the actual libretto, producing it by three stages. First, he would write a rough script containing only the spoken dialogue: the barest outline to carry the action. Next, he would revise, elaborate, introduce jokes and witticisms at suitable places, and revise again. Finally, he would write the songs, and musical items. As soon as the first act was finished, Gilbert would hand this over to Sullivan to compose the music, while he himself got down to the second act.

Gilbert liked to write in peace and quiet, but Sullivan could compose with people bustling around and even talking to him: nothing seemed to disturb his train of thought. Instead of composing at the piano in quiet solitude, as is the custom of many musicians, he would commit his melodies straight onto paper. Seated at his table, smoking endless cigarettes from a long amber cigarette holder, he would first work out his rhythm in dots and dashes, and from this he would gradually build up his score. Sometimes he might take several days to compose a piece of music of only two or three minutes' playing time, but as a rule he worked at great speed.

George Grossmith was spellbound the first time he watched Sullivan compose. "Why, it's like writing shorthand," he remarked as Sullivan's pen slid across the page.

"Yes, but it's quicker," Sullivan replied.

"Do you wait for an inspiration before starting to compose?" Grossmith asked him.

"No, no, my dear fellow, I should seldom compose anything if I were to wait for inspiration," Sullivan snswered, his pen still flashing. "The miner does not sit at the top of the shaft waiting for the coal to come bubbling to the surface! Some days I find work harder than others but Gilbert's librettos are in themselves so inspiring that, once I have got into the theme, I can usually compose in a steady flow."

Gilbert and Sullivan inspired each other, the cast, orchestra, and everyone associated with them. And, now that they had a theater really worthy of them, the "Savoyards," as their company came to be known, became even more popular with the general public.

Patience ran at The Savoy for over a year, making a run of eighteen months altogether, and it earned the partners a small fortune. Gilbert built himself a large new house in South Kensington, and Sullivan moved into a more luxurious apartment in Queen Victoria Street; and both men took a well-deserved holiday. Gilbert went yachting in the English Channel with his wife and a few friends; and Sullivan accompanied the Duke of Edinburgh and other members of the royal family on a cruise around Europe and Asia. During the trip he was introduced to several kings and princes, including the German Kaiser, Wilhelm II, who insisted upon singing the First Lord's song from *H.M.S. Pinafore* to his accompaniment.

Sullivan's obvious delight in his association with royalty and the aristocracy had come to irritate Gilbert. In view of Sullivan's humble background, Gilbert considered this unwarranted snobbery, "social climbing," and, though he tried to hide his feelings, this underlying irritation inevitably imposed another strain on their personal relations. Gilbert was decidedly put out when, on returning from

his own holiday agog to write another opera, he learned
that Sullivan was still in the Baltic and unlikely to be
home again for several more weeks. "All this pandering
to royalty!" he scoffed.

The next opera was to be *Iolanthe*, a skit on the limited
powers of the House of Lords, for whose reform the House
of Commons was then agitating. Nothing seemed to go
right for Sullivan with this opera. He disliked the first act
of the original libretto, and had to ask Gilbert to make
several drastic alterations. Sullivan was pleased with the
revised script, but a few days after receiving it, his mother
died and he became incapable of serious concentration. A
wealthy American, Mrs. Ronalds, with whom he had
formed a close friendship, gradually nursed him out of his
misery, and, with her encouragement, he finally wrote the
music for *Iolanthe*. Sullivan then received another bitter
blow: just as he was leaving home to conduct the opening performance, on the evening of November 25, 1881,
he was handed a letter informing him that his stock-
brokers had gone bankrupt and that he had lost his life's
savings. He bore the news with fortitude, telling no one of
his misfortune until after the performance.

Iolanthe was produced simultaneously in England and
the United States, receiving the usual generous acclaim in
both countries. The Liberal leader, Mr. Gladstone, who
attended the first night at The Savoy, was highly delighted
at this tilt at the House of Lords. Afterward he wrote expressing his appreciation: "so good in taste, so admirable
in execution." He had particularly enjoyed the song by
Lord Mountararat:

> When Wellington thrashed Bonaparte,
> As ev'ry child can tell,
> The House of Peers, throughout the war,
> Did nothing in particular,
> And did it very well . . .

When *Iolanthe* had been running for some six months, the Queen summoned Arthur Sullivan to Windsor Castle and honored him with a knighthood. He was now just forty-one. It was nearly thirty years since he had sung at the royal christening and had told Queen Victoria of his ambition to become a musician. The Queen, recalling this incident, expressed her personal pleasure in bestowing this honor upon him.

CHAPTER TEN

Trial to Triumph

Gilbert, who was to wait another twenty-four years for his knighthood, could not help feeling a little nettled at his partner's success: he considered, quite justifiably, that he and Sullivan deserved equal credit for the popularity of their operas and that therefore he also should have been knighted. Without openly saying so, he attributed Sullivan's distinction to favoritism, resulting from his association with influential people, in particular the royal family—a perhaps understandable suspicion, but one without foundation. In fact, Sullivan, who still composed a good deal of serious music and conducted at important concerts, was given this honor in recognition of his great contribution to music generally, not simply for his work with Gilbert; and expert opinion of the day considered his knighthood richly deserved.

At that time, though this is no longer so, Sullivan was generally regarded as a more accomplished artist than Gilbert, and the music critics had always regretted his "wasting his talents" on comic opera. They now made his knighthood an excuse for appealing to him in print to break his partnership with Gilbert and to devote himself entirely to serious music. "Is it not rather *infra dig* for

Sir Arthur Sullivan to write music for Mr. Gilbert?" asked one musical review.

These scathing articles in praise of Sullivan at the expense of Gilbert developed into a campaign that came perilously near to destroying the Savoy Company. Gilbert, though deeply wounded, suffered in silence, except for an occasional angry outburst to his friends; but Sullivan, whose heart was still in serious music, took notice of these critics and went through agonies of mind debating whether to act upon their advice. In a mood of restless indecision, he composed the music for Gilbert's *Princess Ida*—a blank-verse opera about the problem of the education of girls for whom there were then very few schools—and, when this proved a comparative failure, he finally decided to break with Gilbert.

D'Oyly Carte, to whom he announced his decision, was too astonished to take him seriously. Supposing that Sullivan was simply depressed, he invited him to dinner.

"Now then, what's this nonsense about your giving up comic opera?" he asked jovially.

"There's no nonsense about it," Sullivan replied. "I mean what I say: my partnership with Gilbert is at an end!"

"Rubbish! You're just tired," D'Oyly Carte tried to soothe him. "You have been working too hard, and your kidney has been bothering you. Now the strain is telling and making you see things out of proportion."

"No, no—it's not that," Sullivan broke in. "The fact is— well, I am just sick of it all."

D'Oyly Carte turned grave. "Are you *really* serious in what you are saying?"

"Yes—deadly serious!" Sullivan assured him.

D'Oyly Carte used all his power of persuasion to make him see reason, but Sullivan remained adamant. A few days later he went to the Continent for a holiday, without

bothering to tell Gilbert of his intention to end their partnership. D'Oyly Carte tactfully decided to keep Gilbert
in ignorance for the time being in the hope that the change
of air and scenery might make Sullivan feel different.
After allowing him a few weeks to get rested, he wrote
Sullivan a friendly letter, ignoring their discussion and
suggesting that he and Gilbert should now get down to
writing another opera. When Sullivan replied with a flat
refusal, D'Oyly Carte's patience gave out, and he wrote
back in fury, pointing out that Sullivan was under contract
with Gilbert and himself, and threatening legal action if
he should persist in walking out on them. By the same
mail, he broke the news to Gilbert.

Gilbert, who by now had been rendered still more
crotchety by chronic gout, read D'Oyly Carte's letter with
speechless indignation, and then broke into one of his
tirades, to which his wife had become so accustomed that
she no longer even attempted to placate him. Wisely, he
delayed writing to Sullivan until the following day, when,
having slept off the worst of his anger, he adopted a pained
tone. "I learnt from Carte yesterday, to my unbounded
surprise, that you do not intend to write any more operas
of the class with which you and I have been so long iden-
tified," he wrote. "You have often expatiated to me, and
to others, on the thorough good feeling with which we
have worked together for so many years. Nothing, as far
as I am aware, has occurred to induce you to change your
views on this point, and I am therefore absolutely at a loss
to account for the decision . . ."

Sullivan, normally so considerate of other people's feelings, replied in an offhand manner to the effect that he no
longer held a very high opinion of Gilbert's librettos and
was not prepared to waste any more time on them.

Gilbert, as is so often the way with temperamental people, was capable of surprising self-control and magnanimity

in a real crisis. After this cruel snub, he might himself have
wished to end his relations with Sullivan, but, deeply as he
felt this, Gilbert bottled his pride and suggested their
meeting to iron out their differences as soon as Sullivan
returned from his vacation. By this act, he saved the partnership.

They met at Sullivan's apartment two weeks later, shook
hands, and chatted amicably for two hours. Though they
reached no definite agreement, Sullivan promised to consider further collaboration if Gilbert produced an idea for
an opera that really appealed to him.

Gilbert racked his brain, but could get no inspiration
until one day, in May 1884, while he was sitting in his library, a Japanese sword fell from the wall. There happened to be an important Japanese exhibition in London
that was arousing wide interest in the tastes and fashion of
Japan; and the sudden falling of his sword reminded Gilbert of this. "This is it, the very idea I have been looking
for!" he decided. "I will write a libretto about Japan."

He picked up his pen and outlined his new idea
to Sullivan. "A Japanese piece would afford wonderful
opportunities for picturesque scenery and costumes. Moreover, nothing of the kind has ever been attempted in
England before," he enthused. "How do you feel? Does
this appeal to you?" he asked.

Sullivan replied without hesitation that the idea appealed to him greatly. "I gladly undertake to set it without
further discussing the matter," he promised.

"My dear fellow, I can't tell you how pleased I am!"
Gilbert told his partner.

They decided to call this opera *The Mikado,* and, in
their relief at making up their quarrel, they were exag-
geratedly courteous and considerate to each other at every
stage of the writing and production. Gilbert had to draft

his libretto twelve times before it was entirely to Sullivan's liking, but he showed no trace of irritation.

"I am so sorry to put you to all this trouble," Sullivan kept apologizing.

"No trouble at all, my dear fellow," Gilbert would assure him with good grace. "Your suggestions are extremely valuable."

Never had they worked in quite such harmony.

To atone for the disappointment of *Princess Ida*, they determined to make *The Mikado* their greatest work. The opera, though a fantasy, must capture the atmosphere of Japan in every detail and go as near to perfection as was humanly possible. They studied the history, customs and everyday life of the country, and the etiquette at the court of the emperor, or Mikado—first by reading books, and then, when they had acquired a certain background knowledge, by consulting the Japanese who had come to London for the exhibition.

At great expense, they imported direct from Japan traditional costumes, some over two hundred years old, for two or three of the principal performers, and had copies made for the rest. The Mikado's costume was a faithful reproduction of a magnificent gold-embroidered robe and petticoat of one of the early Japanese emperors.

Gilbert commissioned a Japanese dancer to coach the cast in the correct Japanese mannerisms and postures; how to run with little steps with the toes in the right position; how to manipulate a fan; and other pretty details so important to the illusion in such songs as "Three Little Maids from School":

> Three little maids from school are we,
> Pert as a school-girl well can be,
> Filled to the brim with girlish glee,
> Three little maids from school . . .

The first attempts of the actors to impersonate Japanese caused much merriment. Gilbert joined in the fun at the first two or three rehearsals, but then he became the master sergeant and drilled the cast harder than ever, though his gout prevented his prancing about with his usual agility.

On the opening night, March 14, 1885, Gilbert's agitation was worse than ever. He kept poking his head into the dressing rooms with last-minute instructions and reminders for the actors and actresses.

"For goodness sake, don't make a mistake with your fan!"

"No, Mr. Gilbert, I won't."

"And be sure to get your toes right. Most important!"

"Yes, Mr. Gilbert, I know. Don't worry—I won't let you down."

With a grunt of "good luck!" Gilbert would hobble along to the next dressing room. Having visited each artist once, he fussed about the stage, and then made a second round of the dressing rooms to inquire how the actors and actresses were feeling.

"How do you feel? Are you all right?"

"Yes, thank you, Mr. Gilbert—quite all right."

"Are you sure? . . . You're not nervous?"

Gilbert popped in on one actress so many times that he made her almost hysterical.

"If you ask me again if I feel nervous, I shall scream!" she almost shouted at him. "No, Mr. Gilbert, I am *not* nervous—but you will very soon make me so! For heaven's sake leave me alone!"

Everyone sighed with relief when Gilbert left the theater for his customary walk.

That night, as he stumped up and down the Strand during the performance, was probably the most agonizing of Gilbert's career. "What I suffered during those hours, no man can tell!" he said afterward. But he could have spared himself the anxiety, for *The Mikado* was given a tumultuous reception, and, as Gilbert and Sullivan had hoped, was hailed by the critics as the greatest of all their operas—"altogether on a higher plane," as one critic put it.

The quarrel between Gilbert and Sullivan, so near to finishing their partnership, had ended in their greatest triumph.

The Mikado, which is still one of their most popular operas, ran at The Savoy to a packed house for nearly two years—one of the longest runs of any stage production of the Victorian age.

Meanwhile, American theater managers got busy again. Hearing that one of them, with a view to pirating the opera, was trying to obtain Japanese costumes in London similar to those worn at The Savoy, D'Oyly Carte stepped in smartly and bought up the complete stock of every shop selling Japanese clothes. He also sent a man to Paris to buy up the stocks of the French shops. This was only the first round of the battle, a mere delaying action. "We shall have to fight again, fight the Americans on their own ground," D'Oyly Carte warned his partners.

Gilbert and Sullivan agreed, and decided to forestall the pirates by sending D'Oyly Carte to New York with a second Savoy company to produce their own version of *The Mikado* before any damage could be done. They trained and rehearsed this company in great haste and secrecy, deliberately misleading the artists into thinking that they were to be sent on a tour of the English provincial towns and cities. Then, two days before they were to sail, D'Oyly Carte shepherded them into his private room at The Savoy, locked the door, and finally took them into his confidence. "We are going to America—to New York," he announced simply.

"To *America*!" they gasped as with one breath.

On learning the reason, their enthusiasm mounted.

"You must not breathe a word about this to anyone—not even to your families," D'Oyly Carte warned them. "If news of our intention should leak out, our whole plan might be wrecked!"

The cast respected his confidence; and two days later, on August 7, 1885, the company left London by the midnight train for Liverpool to board a ship for New York. Sullivan, who had relations in the United States whom he was anxious to visit, decided at the last moment to accompany them and to take the opportunity of conducting the orchestra at some of their performances. After breakfasting together at a small commercial hotel in Liverpool, they were taken in a special tug to their liner, before the rest of the passengers could go aboard. They were locked into their cabins until the ship had sailed and there was no longer any risk of their secret being discovered and cabled to America.

The plot succeeded. The Savoyards took New York by storm, and then swept on in triumph to other American towns and cities before the pirates could even get started. Later, the company toured Australia, South Africa, and several European countries, receiving the same wild acclaim wherever they went.

The Mikado had enriched the name and fame of Gilbert and Sullivan in four continents.

CHAPTER ELEVEN

An Opera Is Booed!

When *The Mikado* had been running in London for some nine months, Gilbert had a sudden inspiration to write an opera about an imaginary old Cornish family whose long line of baronets step out of their picture frames and return to life at Ruddigore, their ancestral castle.

The idea came to him while he was dressing one biting cold morning in January 1886, and he thought it so brilliant that he hurried through his breakfast and trudged through the snow on foot, the horse transport having been brought to a standstill by the slippery conditions, to obtain Sullivan's views.

"My dear Gilbert, whatever brings you out in this weather?" Sullivan greeted him, eyeing the drifts of snow on his overcoat.

"I've got an idea! I must tell you about it!" Gilbert blurted out with the impetuosity of a schoolboy.

Sullivan led his partner to his snug study fire, heaped on the coals, and listened in silent amusement as, with mounting enthusiasm, Gilbert poured out his latest brain wave.

"Well, what's your opinion? Do you like it?" Gilbert shot out on finishing.

Sullivan laughed. "It certainly has possibilities. The portraits turning into ghosts should be fun!"

Gilbert beamed. "Yes, I was rather pleased with that . . . I'm glad you approve. I will get down to this immediately."

"No need to hurry," Sullivan observed casually.

"Yes, yes, there is," Gilbert contradicted. 'We must be ready with something good to follow *The Mikado. The Mikado* can't go on forever!"

Sullivan shrugged. "By all means write the libretto, but I fear it may be some time before I can compose the music," he warned his partner, going on to explain that he had just been commissioned to compose a cantata, *The Golden Legend,* for an important music festival to be held at Leeds the following October. "I shall have to give this my undivided attention," he said with finality.

Gilbert was crestfallen, but forced a smile. "I see . . . Well, I suppose I shall have to be patient! But don't take too long over this—this other business," he urged, trying to hide his irritation.

It was a long time before Sullivan even began to compose *The Golden Legend* as he had a sudden lazy streak when he did no work at all. During the next three months or so, he spent most of his time gadding about, attending the races and playing cards at the homes of the aristocracy; and generally hobnobbing with the nobility. Then, as a further distraction, Liszt paid an unexpected visit to England. Sullivan, who had not seen the Hungarian pianist since their one meeting at Leipzig during his student days, joyfully renewed their acquaintance and introduced him to London society in the hope of arousing interest in his music, and, as with the music of Schubert and Schumann, he met with considerable success.

Gilbert, who had written and delivered the libretto of *Ruddigore* without receiving so much as an acknowledgment, was furious when it came to his ears that his partner had taken a break from composing. Hesitating to speak his

mind for fear of causing a final rift in their partnership, he
paid Sullivan an ostensibly friendly visit and tried to stir
him into action by inquiring as to the progress he was making with his cantata.

"Have you much more to write?" he asked affably. "I
expect you have nearly finished it by now."

"Finished? I haven't started yet!" Sullivan replied airily.

Gilbert kept up the pretense. "Really? That's surprising. What has been the trouble?"

"I just haven't felt like composing—that's all!" Sullivan
answered almost tartly.

His casual attitude infuriated Gilbert, but he kept control of his temper, and laughingly hinted that Sullivan
might find progress easier if only he were to exert himself
a little harder. "If the Muse does not come to you, you
must woo her!"

This remark caught Sullivan on the raw. "What do you
take me for, a barrel organ?" he snapped.

It was useless to press the issue any further. Nevertheless, Gilbert's gentle prodding bore fruit, for a few weeks
later Sullivan rented a cottage in the country, where he
would be away from the temptation to idle in social activities, and at last made a start on his cantata. After wasting
two months dabbling with various themes only to tear
them up, inspiration came; and he then worked for seven
weeks at a stretch, snatching hasty meals, making do with
very little sleep, and in almost constant pain from his kidney disease.

When the score was finished, Sullivan collapsed, reviv-
ing only just in time to conduct *The Golden Legend* at
the Leeds Festival, where it was given a magnificent reception, surpassing anything Sullivan had experienced pre-
viously. As he turned from the orchestra to bow to the
audience, the applause was thunderous, and many people
in the stalls ran forward to pelt him with flowers. The

critics were equally appreciative, one musical review now calling him "the Mozart of England." Queen Victoria, one of the first people to congratulate him, said: "Perhaps one day, Sir Arthur, you will compose a grand opera. You would do it so well."

Gilbert added his congratulations by letter, with a gentle reminder that the music for *Ruddigore* still awaited his attention. Sullivan responded to his appeal with another burst of feverish activity, making up for his dilatoriness by composing *Ruddigore* in record time.

Sullivan considered, with possible justification, this music, on the whole, the best he had yet written for light opera. Gilbert held the same opinion about his libretto. Each was delighted with his own efforts but did not think so highly of his partner's. The perfect blending of libretto and music, for which they had been praised so often, somehow seemed to be lacking in *Ruddigore*. Gilbert blamed the music for this, and Sullivan blamed the libretto. But neither dared express his criticism openly to the other for fear of causing irreparable offense, so strained had their relations grown by now. So, quite independently, they took a mutual friend into their confidence and requested him to pass on their views as though they were his own.

"Though to my uninstructed ear," Gilbert commented, "nothing could be better than the music, there is so much of it that I am afraid the audience will lose the thread of the story, and forget what it is all about! Perhaps you could suggest to Sullivan that if one or two numbers were cut, the piece would play more briskly."

Sullivan asked the friend how he thought the piece was shaping, and, without giving him the chance to reply, went on to observe: "It is supposed to be an opera but it is really becoming a play with a few songs and some concerted music. Don't you think it would be as well to hint to Gilbert that the music is disappearing into the background?"

These tactics were of no avail; and when the curtain fell on the opening performance of *Ruddigore*, on January 22, 1887, Gilbert and Sullivan, for the first time in their career, suffered the indignity of hearing their opera hissed and booed by a section of the audience. Most of the critics praised Sullivan's music, and several paid tribute to the quality of Gilbert's production, upon which he had spent about £8,000 ($40,000); but it was the general opinion that *Ruddigore* was "not half as good" as *The Mikado*.

Though the opera was to run for about twelve months, earning each partner about £7,000 ($35,000), Gilbert and Sullivan condemned it as a failure and began to indulge in painful recriminations. They still harbored their grievances instead of expressing them openly, but each sensed how the other felt, and inevitably this created an undercurrent of hostility.

The position became so intolerable that, throughout the spring and summer of 1887, they met only when absolutely necessary, when they had something of vital importance to discuss. Sullivan devoted himself to setting to music an ode by Tennyson in commemoration of Queen Victoria's Golden Jubilee, in June of that year—a work, commissioned by the Prince of Wales, that raised Sullivan's stock with the royal family still higher. "The Queen is delighted with it," the Prince told Sullivan, who celebrated this latest success with another hectic round of social enjoyment.

Gilbert, meanwhile, buried himself in a rented house in a village near London, toying with various ideas for an opera to succeed *Ruddigore,* but made no headway.

Finally, in the autumn, Gilbert and Sullivan, feeling by now less edgy with each other, met and agreed to replace *Ruddigore* with a revival of *H.M.S. Pinafore* as a stopgap —the first time they had run dry and resorted to a revival.

One day when Gilbert went to The Savoy to rehearse

H.M.S. Pinafore, D'Oyly Carte met him in a corridor and pointed to the shabby condition of the carpet outside the room which he shared with Sullivan. "It's beginning to look a bit shoddy. See, it's worn through!" he said.

Gilbert grunted.

"You might consider buying yourself a new carpet," D'Oyly Carte went on. "With the colossal royalties you are earning, you could surely spare a few pounds on a carpet!"

This remark, though made in jest, infuriated Gilbert.

"Why the devil should I buy a carpet?" he flashed. "It's not my responsibility! Buy one yourself!"

Stung by Gilbert's ungovernable temper, D'Oyly Carte stopped chiding and retorted heatedly: "The room is used by you and Sullivan and therefore the carpet *is* your responsibility."

"Then make Sullivan pay for it!" Gilbert roared, adding bitterly: "He makes far more money than I do! His music is *much* superior to my humble librettos! Ask the critics . . ."

Unhappily, Sullivan walked in just as Gilbert was making this sarcastic jibe, with the result that what had been intended as a harmless piece of chaff flared into a furious row among all three partners.

Their quarrel gradually blew over and, as before, Gilbert and Sullivan became unnaturally polite and courteous to each other. Several weeks later, when they went to The Savoy for another rehearsal of *H.M.S. Pinafore,* Gilbert announced joyfully that at last he had thought of a good idea for a new opera.

"It came to me in a flash while I was waiting for a train at Uxbridge station," he told Sullivan. "I suddenly noticed a poster of a beefeater in the colorful uniform of a

Yeoman of the Guard, with the Tower of London in the background."

Sullivan's eyes lit up. "You, you are thinking of an opera about the Tower of London?"

"Exactly, my dear fellow! Think of all the romance and tradition, the history and pageantry, we could weave in!" Gilbert enthused.

The Yeoman of the Guard, as Gilbert eventually decided to call this opera, was to be a departure from his usual topsy-turvydom, and on this account the idea appealed greatly to Sullivan. For some time, he had been urging Gilbert to write a libretto that would allow him to introduce greater dignity into his music, and this seemed to be the answer. "Now this really is a good idea, first rate," he said.

Gilbert spent days and weeks at the Tower of London, studying the history and capturing the atmosphere of this historic building, paying the same close attention to detail as he had when writing *The Mikado*. He then framed his story in close consultation with Sullivan and, having obtained his approval on every point, began work on the actual libretto.

Everything ran smoothly, until, just as he was finishing the libretto, Gilbert received a letter from Sullivan begging off. Sullivan, on vacation at Monte Carlo, had been spending his time at the Casino and debating his future. A mood of idle restlessness, aggravated by his losing money at the tables, he had decided, for the second time, that he was wasting his talents at comic opera and must henceforth devote himself exclusively to serious music. There was to be no more turning back. His decision was quite final, he told Gilbert.

Gilbert was shocked beyond anger. "I can't, for the life of me," he replied, "understand the reasons that urge you to abandon a theater and a company that have worked so well for us, and for whom we have worked so well. Why in the world are we to throw up the sponge? . . . We have the best theater, the best company, the best composer, and (though I say it) the best librettist in England working together—we are world-known and as much an institution as Westminster Abbey—and to scatter this splendid organization is, to my way of thinking, to give up a gold mien."

Sullivan, easily influenced, saw reason and changed his mind. Within two or three weeks, he was at work on *The Yeoman of the Guard.*

The music did not come as easily as he had anticipated; the song, "I have a song to sing, O!" caused him unusual difficulty. Night after night, Sullivan lay awake puzzling how to set it. One morning, when a friend called to see him, he greeted him by blurting out: "My dear fellow, I have a song to set, O!, and I don't know how the dickens I am going to do it!" After laboring in vain for two weeks on this one song, Sullivan turned in desperation to Gilbert.

"For goodness sake, hum me something," he entreated him.

Gilbert gaped. "Me, hum! Only a rash man ever asks me to hum! Why, I only know two tunes: one's 'God Save the Queen,' and the other isn't!"

Sullivan laughed. "I know your voice is appalling, but never mind that! You have often told me that you have some particular tune in your mind to prompt the meter of a song, so I presume some old air must have prompted this song."

"Yes, it did," Gilbert agreed. "It was an old sea shanty. The sailors . . ."

"Fine! Then hum it to me," Sullivan broke in. "It may help me."

Gilbert croaked a dozen or so bars without striking a single correct note, but his unmelodious effort gave Sullivan the theme he had been seeking. "That's it, I've got it!" he exclaimed exuberantly.

Sullivan set the song to music that very same day, and it became, and has remained, one of the most popular of the songs from *The Yeoman of the Guard.*

In his anxiety to make the opera a success, Gilbert kept pruning and altering to the very last moment. A few hours before the opening performance, on October 3, 1888, he decided that the first scene was sluggish and insisted upon cutting some of the words and music—an idea to which Sullivan gave grudging consent. Still Gilbert was not quite satisfied, and, shortly before the curtain rose, he sent several of the actors and actresses into a dither by rewording some of their lines.

It was surprising that the cast managed to keep their heads with all this fidgeting and fussing, but their team-work was as brilliant and scintillating as ever; and *The Yeoman of the Guard* was adjudged a success.

CHAPTER TWELVE

Their Last Success

In 1888 D'Oyly Carte decided to enter the field of grand opera and to build himself an opera house which he hoped would rival Covent Garden. He invited Sullivan to compose the first grand opera to be produced there. Sullivan by now had a burning ambition to embark upon a work of this kind, and, remembering the Queen's words of encouragement—"You would do it so well"—he accepted this commission with the greatest pleasure.

Sullivan sensed that Gilbert, who was inclined to regard his serious compositions as irritating interruptions to their joint work, might not approve of his decision. And to avoid further unpleasantness, he tactfully invited his partner around to his apartment and suggested that Gilbert write the libretto—in the conviction that Gilbert would refuse!

"This is a splendid opportunity, just what I have been looking for," Sullivan said, after informing Gilbert of D'Oyly Carte's plan. "Light opera may bring in the money, but, well, it's not in the same class as grand opera. I want to go in for serious dramatic work on a large scale, and to compose no more light music. But don't misunderstand me, Gilbert, I have no wish to end our partnership. There is no reason why we should not collaborate at grand opera with the same success as we have had in the past, perhaps with more success. To come to the point, would you care to write the libretto for my new work?"

Gilbert was so taken aback that he was at a loss for words. He nodded in apparent assent, made a few pleasantries, and hurriedly departed. Sullivan now found himself in an embarrassing situation: he did not consider Gilbert a suitable author for this type of libretto, but, if he were to withdraw his invitation, Gilbert would take umbrage and start another violent quarrel. What was he to do? Gilbert solved his problem by having second thoughts on the subject.

He came to the conclusion that grand opera was not really in his line, and wrote to tell Sullivan of his decision. He further doubted whether it would be possible to collect a cast of first-class singers with the ability to act, which he considered essential for this type of production. He did not like the site chosen for D'Oyly Carte's new opera house, and, still more important, he was not prepared to undertake a work where his words would obviously be of second importance to Sullivan's music. "I can quite understand your desire to write a big work," Gilbert wrote in conclusion. "Well, why not write one? But why abandon the Savoy business? Cannot the two things be done concurrently?"

Sullivan, now holidaying with the Prince of Wales at Monte Carlo, was in no mood to be dictated to by Gilbert as to how he should conduct his career. He had a tendency to become rather high and mighty when moving in royal circles, and he became extremely haughty on this occasion. Dropping all pretense at desiring Gilbert's good will, he replied in a lordly tone. "In every single opera we have written to date my music has been sacrificed to your words. So it is surely not unreasonable to expect you to make a similar sacrifice now."

Gilbert dismissed the insult by replying with dignity

that if Sullivan was seriously under the impression that he had been effacing himself during the twelve years of their partnership, there seemed little point in their considering further collaboration.

Angered by this snub, deserved though it was, Sullivan promptly wrote in high dudgeon to D'Oyly Carte, pouring out numerous grossly exaggerated grievances against Gilbert, which he claimed to have bottled up manfully in the interest of the operas ever since they first went into partnership. He accused Gilbert of writing rubbishy librettos unworthy of his music; and of consistently disregarding his opinions and wishes; of overworking the actors and actresses, and wasting everyone's time at rehearsals by unnecessary detail; and of making himself generally objectionable by his egotism, rudeness and bullying. In short, he accused Gilbert of riding roughshod over himself, the cast, and everyone remotely connected with the operas, down to the charwomen at The Savoy.

D'Oyly Carte, normally so shrewd, immediately forwarded Sullivan's letter to Gilbert. The reason for this extraordinary indiscretion will always be a mystery. It has been suggested that D'Oyly Carte himself may have revolted against Gilbert's autocracy and felt this to be a good way of deflating him. Alternatively, in view of the constant friction between the partners, he may have thought it good policy to provoke a first-class row and finally bring matters to a head, whether for good or ill. On the other hand, he may have considered the termination of their partnership inevitable, and decided, in his own interest, to support Sullivan, to ensure his continued co-operation in the new grand-opera venture.

Whatever D'Oyly Carte's motive may have been, the result was inevitable: Gilbert and Sullivan had another and more bitter quarrel. But it cleared the air. After an embittered correspondence lasting several weeks, they met in London for a long and frank discussion of their differences, and, in the words of Sullivan, "shook hands and buried the hatchet."

A month later, in May 1889, Gilbert called on Sullivan with the outline of a new opera, *The Gondoliers,* a story set in Venice. In Victorian times, only the well-to-do went abroad for their vacations, and people who could afford foreign travel felt a certain sense of superiority over the rest of society. About the middle of the century, the author and critic John Ruskin, one of the leaders of the Aesthetic Movement, had visited and written a book about the splendor of Venice; and ever since its publication it had become increasingly fashionable among the upper and middle classes to holiday at this lovely old Italian town, and to sail down the Grand Canal in a gondola. With his eye for topicality, Gilbert directed his wit at this social snobbery, as he considered it, in a satire of great charm and beauty; and Sullivan, who himself had been to Venice earlier in the year, thought his story both "funny and very pretty."

The two partners worked together on *The Gondoliers* in the same perfect harmony as they had written and composed *The Mikado* after their earlier quarrel. When sending his songs to Sullivan to compose the music, Gilbert would enclose a friendly note, saying; "If the verses won't do, send them back, and I'll try again." And, if Sullivan had any criticism to make, he was careful to couch it in a way that could give no possible grounds for offense or misunderstanding. Each went out of his way to meet the other's ideas and wishes. Neither Gilbert nor Sullivan found *The Gondoliers* easy to construct. It took them longer to write than any of their previous works, but never an angry word nor even a trace of irritation passed between them.

The only incident to disturb their serenity occurred at

the first rehearsal, when the cast demanded a rise in salary. Gilbert turned down their demand outright, but Jessie Bond, who was to play the part of Tessa, stood firm, threatening to walk out unless she were paid an extra £10 ($50) a week. When Gilbert explained that, much as he admired her talents, he did not feel justified in raising her salary, Jessie Bond appealed to Sullivan and D'Oyly Carte, both of whom considered her request perfectly reasonable.

With nervous hesitation, Sullivan sidled up to Gilbert at an opportune moment, and broached the subject to him in his most ingratiating manner. "Of course, you are the best judge of these things," he said, "but, you know, Gilbert, I can't help thinking we might be wise to pay Jessie the extra money. After all, she's our best actress. I mean, well, don't you think we might regret her leaving the cast?"

Gilbert gave in but with a far from good grace. His pride wounded at having to submit to the dictates of an actress, he refused to address a single word to Jessie, except to correct her, throughout the rehearsals; once, when she came on to the stage, he called out sarcastically: "Make way for the high-salaried artiste!"

But he bore her no real malice, and, at the end of the final dress rehearsal, he surprised everyone by hobbling on to the stage with his stick—upon which his gout had now made him dependent—and giving her a bearlike hug, exclaimed with gusto: "Jessie, my dear, I had no idea that so much could be made of so small a part!"

The Gondoliers, first produced at The Savoy on December 7, 1889, had the most glorious first night of all the operas, the ovation ringing down the Strand above the clip-clop of the horses drawing the carriages and omnibuses. When Gilbert and Sullivan appeared before the curtain to acknowledge the acclaim, they were so moved by their reception that tears welled in their eyes. So great was their emotion, indeed, that they left the theater that night with hardly a word to each other, not daring to express their feelings lest they should break down.

Next morning, Gilbert wrote Sullivan a charming little note: "I must thank you again for the magnificent work you have put into the piece. It gives one the chance of shining right through the twentieth century with a reflected light."

Sullivan, deeply touched, replied graciously: "Don't talk of reflected light. In such a perfect book as *The Gondoliers* you shine with an individual brilliancy that no other writer can hope to attain. If any thanks are due anywhere, they should be from me to you for the patience, willingness, and unfailing good nature with which you have received my suggestions, and your readiness to help me by according to them."

Both these tributes came from the heart. Like many of the critics, Gilbert and Sullivan considered *The Gondoliers* their crowning glory, and each recognized how much he owed to his partner for its success.

It was their last success.

CHAPTER THIRTEEN

A Quarrel Over a Carpet

The serenity between the partners was shattered abruptly when Gilbert received from D'Oyly Carte an account for £4,500 ($22,500) for his and Sullivan's share of the expenses of *The Gondoliers* for the first three months of its run.

The running costs of The Savoy, amounting to about £130 ($650) a performance, had caused Gilbert some concern ever since the opening of the theater. From time to time, he had suggested to D'Oyly Carte that these expenses might be reduced, but, as Sullivan had not seen eye to eye with him over this and had refused to be drawn into their discussions, Gilbert had not pressed the issue. However, the expenses of *The Gondoliers* seemed so stupendous that he demanded to be sent a detailed report as to how this figure had been reached.

On receipt of this, Gilbert noted with amazement that a sum of £500 ($2,500) had been charged for new carpeting for the front of the theater: for the auditorium, stairs and corridors. Since their agreement with D'Oyly Carte rendered Gilbert and Sullivan liable only for "repairs incidental to the performances," Gilbert tersely requested an explanation. D'Oyly Carte replied vindictively, dodging the question and virtually telling Gilbert to mind his own business, adding that both he and Sullivan were tired of his perpetual interference in matters that really were no concern of his.

Incensed at his highhanded attitude, Gilbert stormed into D'Oyly Carte's office at The Savoy to thrash out the matter with him in person.

"Do you think I'm going to pay for a confounded carpet for the stairs to an office where you do the dirty business of your blasted opera house?" he fumed.

D'Oyly Carte seethed. "Withdraw that remark immediately!"

"I shall do no such thing until I have an explanation of your extraordinary conduct," Gilbert shouted.

D'Oyly Carte retorted that his conduct was not in the least extraordinary. "You and Sullivan are jointly liable for two-thirds of the cost of all the upholstery in the front of the theater, and it is on this basis that I am charging you £500 for this carpet. The actual price of the carpet is £750, and I shall be paying the remaining third of the cost."

"That's generous of you—most generous!" Gilbert scoffed.

"No need to be offensive!"

"Well, I don't intend to pay anything, not a penny!" Gilbert went on. "Under our agreement, Sullivan and I are responsible only for repairs connected with the performances, and new carpets cannot possibly come under the heading of repairs. At that rate, you might just as well expect us to pay for redecorating the theater, and for all your other confounded commitments!"

D'Oyly Carte refused to give ground, arguing that Gilbert was misinterpreting the relevant clause in their contract. "The charge is perfectly legitimate, and nothing will induce me to accept your interpretation."

"Then why," asked Gilbert, "did you not consult Sullivan and myself before involving us in this enormous expense? If, as you contend, this confounded carpet is our liability, then you should most certainly have obtained our permission before buying it." He added bitterly: "Since these furnishings are legally your property, you seem to be coming out of this deal very nicely!"

D'Oyly Carte glowered, and made no reply.

"I refuse to write a new piece for The Savoy unless a fresh agreement is drawn up," Gilbert threatened.

"If you are dissatisfied, you have only to say so," D'Oyly Carte baited him with studied calmness.

"I am dissatisfied!" Gilbert roared.

D'Oyly Carte smiled cynically and said: "Very well, then, you write no more for The Savoy, that's understood."

Interpreting this as a dismissal, Gilbert hurled abuse at D'Oyly Carte. "It is a mistake to kick down the ladder by which you have risen," he scoffed. "Sullivan and I have raised you from penury to affluence by our operas, and you will do well to remember this!"

With that parting shot, he stormed out of the room, slamming the door behind him.

Sullivan was at Monte Carlo again at the time of this interview, but, on his return, Gilbert gave him a full report of what had occurred. To his dismay, Sullivan seemed to think he was making a lot of fuss about nothing. Sullivan's mind was on his grand opera, which he had now begun to write, and he had no wish to fall out with D'Oyly Carte about a mere £500 for a carpet. The matter was too trivial. For the sake of peace, Sullivan agreed to act as mediator by arranging a further meeting between Gilbert and D'Oyly Carte to smooth out the trouble, but, in spite of several promptings from Gilbert, he, in fact, did nothing.

Finally, Gilbert, feeling that Sullivan was letting him down, resorted to shock tactics by serving both him and

D'Oyly Carte with notices of his intention to terminate their partnership at the end of the year. "The time for putting an end to our collaboration has at last arrived," he wrote to Sullivan. "I am writing a letter to Carte (of which I enclose a copy) giving him notice that he is not to produce or perform any of my librettos after Christmas 1890 . . . After the withdrawal of *The Gondoliers,* our united work will be heard in public no more."

This resolute act jolted them to their senses. Both Sullivan and D'Oyly Carte had themselves threatened to end the partnership in moments of anger or frustration, but they had not expected Gilbert to do so. Mortified at his obvious intention to carry out his threat, they pocketed their pride and invited him to meet them at The Savoy for a friendly discussion. Gilbert agreed.

But they were not in a fit condition for amicable discussion. Gilbert's feet were swollen and red with gout, which was driving him nearly mad; Sullivan was seldom out of pain from his kidney complaint; and D'Oyly Carte was tired and strained from overwork and in danger of a breakdown.

Inevitably, another heated argument, on the lines of the first, soon blew up between Gilbert and D'Oyly Carte.

"I repeat," shouted Gilbert, "that these expenses are unwarrantable and excessive. You are making far too much money out of my brains, and I demand a fresh agreement before I write another word."

After ranting and shouting at each other for close to half an hour, with neither man yielding an inch, Gilbert suddenly turned to Sullivan, who had sat in silence, and appealed for his support. "This affects you just as much as me! For God's sake, back me up!"

To Gilbert's utter disgust, Sullivan sided with D'Oyly Carte. "I'm sorry, Gilbert, but I just cannot agree with you. I think Carte is in the right over these expenses."

Gilbert rose from his chair in fury, "What!" he roared. "You take Carte's part! . . . You are no gentleman! . . . You are blackguards—both of you!"

With a torrent of unprintable language, he stumped across to the door, wrenched it open, and crashed out of the room, shouting: "I'll beat you yet, you—cheats!"

The following day, his temper not improved by a restless night of gout, Gilbert wrote Sullivan an irate letter, demanding a full apology for his "hostile" attitude, and insisting upon his breaking off relations with D'Oyly Carte immediately. Sullivan, refusing to be browbeaten, replied that Gilbert's behavior had been outrageous, and that it was for him to do the apologizing.

Gilbert, as was his custom when he failed to get his way, now put the matter into the hands of his lawyers. He instructed them to inspect the theater accounts during the past few years, and he had the effrontery to appeal to Sullivan to uphold him in the event of D'Oyly Carte's raising objections. Sullivan, not surprisingly, refused his request. "I have no grievance, no dispute," he declared, adding: "The deplorable step of calling in lawyer and accountant has rendered a satisfactory settlement almost impossible. My object now is to do nothing that will add fuel to the fire, and consequently I hold entirely aloof from taking part in this unhappy dispute . . ."

D'Oyly Carte, as expected, refused permission for the books to be inspected, but the lawyers detected a serious discrepancy in the recent accounts submitted to Gilbert. Suspecting, though without any grounds for this suspicion, that D'Oyly Carte might be withholding money to help pay for his new opera house, Gilbert promptly made legal application for the appointment of an official receiver to take charge of the finances of The Savoy Theatre, but D'Oyly Carte successfully resisted this, with the aid of a testimony from Sullivan. Refusing to be thwarted, Gilbert now brought a legal action against both his partners, charging them, in effect, with bearing false testimony, and claiming £1,000 ($5,000) from D'Oyly Carte, which he alleged had been withheld from his share of the company's profits.

This action, the first public indication of a serious breach between the partners, came as a bombshell to the countless lovers of the Gilbert and Sullivan operas, who were still flocking nightly to The Savoy to see *The Gondoliers.* Was it possible that this superb partnership of composer and librettist, famous all over the world, could collapse over a mere carpet?

The case, which aroused wide interest, was heard early in September 1890. Though no mention of fraud was made or even suggested, D'Oyly Carte's action in withholding money due to Gilbert caused a most unfavorable impression, and he was ordered to pay the £1,000 claim forthwith.

Having won his case, Gilbert triumphantly tried to make peace with his partners. He wrote to Sullivan, dismissing their quarrel as a really quite trifling matter, but Sullivan could not bring himself to treat it so lightly.

"I am only human," he replied, "and I confess frankly that I am still smarting under a sense of the unjust and ungenerous treatment I have received at your hands . . . With the scandal of last Wednesday's proceedings still vividly before me, I could not sit down and discuss the original dispute calmly . . . Don't think me exaggerating when I tell you that I am physically and mentally ill over this wretched business. I have not yet got over the shock of seeing our names coupled, not in brilliant collaboration over a work destined for world-wide celebrity, but in hostile antagonism over a few miserable pounds . . ."

Gilbert also appealed to Mrs. D'Oyly Carte to use her

influence to bring about a reconciliation between himself and her husband, confessing that he had spoken in anger and probably said many things that were most unfair, but assuring her that he no longer bore any ill will. Mrs. D'Oyly Carte generously agreed to see what she could do. But then Gilbert undid all the good by following up his peace overtures with a demand for the accounts of the company, for the whole period of their partnership, to be examined by a legal expert.

Both D'Oyly Carte and Sullivan were disgusted. "I thought that bygones were to be bygones, and that no further reference was to be made to any of the matters lately in dispute," wrote Sullivan. "Surely, my dear Gilbert," he appealed to him, "you can afford to let things rest as they are now, and let us forget the past."

Gilbert, who was earning between £10,000 ($50,000) and £14,000 ($70,000) a year from his operas, certainly could have afforded to drop the matter from the financial point of view, but he was determined to prosecute it to the bitter end on a point of principle. And so the quarrel flared up again. During the next few weeks, the partners met two or three times to try to reach an amicable settlement of their dispute, but on each occasion the wretched carpet came between them, and they broke up with shouting and banging of fists on the table.

Finally, after quarreling for just over a year, D'Oyly Carte went to Gilbert and apologetically confessed to certain "errors" in the accounts. "He has admitted," Gilbert reported to Sullivan, "an unintentional overcharge of nearly £1,000 in the electric-lighting accounts alone. He also admits that there are other items charged in the disputed accounts which should not have been charged, and he expresses his readiness to put these matters right as soon as *The Gondoliers* is withdrawn."

Regarding this as a moral victory, Gilbert now let the matter drop; and the three men patched up their quarrel. But their wounds had gone too deep for their relationship to return to normal, and Gilbert and Sullivan agreed to go their separate ways.

CHAPTER FOURTEEN

Swan Song

Throughout the long months of their quarrel, Sullivan had been plugging away doggedly at his grand opera, having chosen as his subject Sir Walter Scott's romantic novel *Ivanhoe*. Though distracted by Gilbert's bitter attacks on him and by the unpleasant publicity attending the legal action against D'Oyly Carte and himself, he had completed this work, which meant more to him than anything he had written, by January 1891. The conditions under which he had been obliged to compose might have taxed the greatest genius. Somehow, though how he did not know, Sullivan had managed to put his worries into the back of his mind while at work and to acquire that deep concentration so necessary in creative work, and in consequence the opera turned out much better than he himself had expected. Indeed, he felt that he had produced a masterpiece, and so did D'Oyly Carte.

With visions of his new operatic center becoming the talk of London, of England and perhaps of the world, D'Oyly Carte spent a fortune on the production of *Ivanhoe*, and launched a sensational publicity campaign, suggesting, though without actually saying so, that Sullivan's new opera was the equal of, or even better than, Gounod's

Faust and the great operatic masterpieces of Wagner and Mozart.

As was the intention, this blaze of exaggerated publicity drew the cream of London society—princes and princesses, dukes and duchesses, peers and peeresses—to the opening of the new opera house. People with not a note of music in them bought seats as eagerly as true music-lovers, simply because they considered this an important social occasion calling for their attendance.

Sullivan had hoped that Gilbert, in spite of his dislike of high-quality music, might honor him with his presence, but Gilbert still harbored an undercurrent of grievance, and felt unable to accept the invitation. "I decline your stalls," he wrote. However, the Prince and Princess of Wales and the Duke and Duchess of Edinburgh attended, which was most gratifying.

The distinguished audience showed immense enthusiasm for Sullivan's grand opera, their acclaim far surpassing both his and D'Oyly Carte's highest expectations. Since so few of them possessed any real love or knowledge of music, the volume of their applause was surprising, but the critics were also eulogistic, proclaiming *Ivanhoe* Sullivan's greatest composition, and declaring that D'Oyly Carte's entry into the field of grand opera marked a new era for serious music. The hundreds of congratulatory letters that were showered upon Sullivan during the next few days and weeks included one from Queen Victoria expressing "particular satisfaction" because, as she said, "she believes it is partly owing to her own instigation that you undertook this great work." Sullivan smiled with pride and gratitude on reading this letter, and, in thanking the Queen, he asked her permission to dedicate *Ivanhoe* to her in grateful acknowledgment of her influence, a gesture that touched the Queen deeply.

Sullivan now felt on top of the world, but his latest triumph was short-lived. Gilbert had been right in his contention that grand opera would have no lasting appeal in England, and the critics wrong in their belief that a new era for serious music had begun. The British had not been educated to grand opera, and, after the first flush, their enthusiasm waned. The audience began to dwindle with almost every performance until, after five months, *Ivanhoe* was withdrawn.

Sullivan was mortified. "This is the greatest disappointment of my career," he told a friend, who passed on the remark to Gilbert. Having warned Sullivan of the likelihood of this, Gilbert, though sorry for anyone whose dream was shattered, could feel no great sympathy for him. "He sits on a fire and then complains that his bottom is burning!" he observed.

D'Oyly Carte, having suffered a serious financial loss on his grandiose venture, now sold his splendid new opera house to a music-hall company, abandoned forever his dream of establishing grand opera in England, and returned to comic opera, in association with Arthur Sullivan.

Sullivan and D'Oyly Carte, who were lost without Gilbert, though they would never admit it, spent the next eighteen months or so flitting like bees from one flowery idea to another without gathering much honey. Sullivan composed the music for a libretto, *Hadden Hall,* by Sydney Grundy, but the words did not inspire him as Gilbert's libretto had done; and the opera had only a very short run.

With his knack for spotting new talent, D'Oyly Carte unearthed a promising young writer, James Barrie, who a few years later was to make his name with *Peter Pan,* and suggested that Sullivan might consider collaborating with him.

"I think he will go far," D'Oyly Carte prophesied. "Read this, and see what you think of it," he invited Sullivan, handing him a sample of Barrie's work.

Sullivan read the libretto, but was not impressed. "Sorry, Carte, but I cannot share your enthusiasm. This scenario is teeming with faults. I am sure I could never work with this librettist, it would be useless to try," he declared with finality.

D'Oyly Carte then sought out a dramatic critic who was to achieve world fame as a playwright, George Bernard Shaw; but, as Sullivan and Shaw did not take to each other, nothing came of that introduction either.

Worn to a frazzle by this frustration on top of his bitter quarrel with Gilbert, which by now was simmering dangerously near to the boil again, Sullivan had a serious breakdown in the spring of 1892. For several weeks, he hovered between life and death in a state of semi-consciousness, with the doctor deadening the excruciating pain from his kidney with frequent injections of morphine. In his few moments of full consciousness, Sullivan felt convinced that he was dying, and rumors to this effect began to be reported in the newspapers.

The Queen and the royal family, like his countless other admirers throughout the country, were deeply distressed on reading of this; and the Prince of Wales immediately sent his personal physician to examine Sullivan. The physician expressed the opinion that only a serious operation could save Sullivan's life, but that he was too weak to survive such an operation. "I am afraid there is no hope," he reported to the Prince, but he was wrong.

A few days later, Sullivan's nephew, Herbert, his dead brother Frederick's son, whom he had come to love as dearly as if he were his own son, was sitting at the dying composer's bedside, when he thought of giving his uncle a piping-hot bath. No doubt the doctors would have protested that such treatment was more likely to kill than cure, but, in view of Sullivan's apparently hopeless condition, Herbert considered this risk justified. With the help of the valet, he gently lowered his uncle into the bathtub, and almost immediately he began to make a miraculous recovery.

Gilbert spent these eighteen months likewise dabbling with other composers. He produced one opera, *The Mountebanks,* that proved fairly popular, but, though he met with rather more success on his own than did Sullivan, he, too, felt at sea without his old partner.

Now, as never before, both Gilbert and Sullivan had come to appreciate how much each had owed to the other for their brilliant successes of the past. No one could give either of them the inspiration they had drawn from each other, and yet they could not bring themselves completely to forgive and forget and join forces again.

Eventually the music publisher, Tom Chappell, believing that only false pride was keeping them apart, appealed to Gilbert to bury his nagging grievances and to pick up the tattered threads. "I beg of you both to work together again," he pleaded. "Is there *no* possibility of this?"

"I fear not," Gilbert told him. "Neither of us will ever be able to forget all that has passed between us. Sullivan and I each feel unjustly treated by the other, and, so long as that is so, it is impossible to recapture the cordial understanding so necessary between two men working in collaboration."

"But surely, my dear Gilbert," Chappell pressed him, "you and Sullivan could heal your wounds with a little give-and-take on both sides. That is all that is required."

But Gilbert remained adamant. "The position is hopeless," he repeated.

Refusing to accept this as final, Chappell called on Gilbert again a few days later for some gentle coaxing. He then went to see Sullivan, who welcomed his efforts at mediation, and responded to his appeal by dropping Gilbert a short, friendly note, suggesting: "Let us meet and shake hands." To show good will, he added jocularly: "We can dispel the cloud hanging over us by setting up a counterirritant in the form of a cloud of smoke!"

Gilbert would have been incapable of writing to Sullivan in this vein because he would have been afraid of having his overture mistaken for meek submission, but, now that his partner had made the first move, he was willing to accept his olive branch. Thus, early in 1893, Gilbert and Sullivan buried the hatchet once more and settled down to writing another opera together, *Utopia Limited*.

Sullivan was pleased to be working with Gilbert again. "After all," he remarked to a friend, "there's nobody like him!" Gilbert, though more hesitant to admit the fact, felt the same way about Sullivan. The courteous behavior that had followed their previous quarrels was again in evidence, but this time it did not last.

D'Oyly Carte caused the first upset by estimating the production costs of *Utopia Limited* at about £7,000 ($35,000). Surprisingly, Gilbert, so often his critic, thought this quite reasonable but Sullivan, his champion, considered the figure excessive, and pressed for a rigid economy in the costumes. At this, Gilbert was incensed, protesting, "Gents in Arms must be dressed somehow! They can't go naked, unless, of course, you insist upon this!"

Sullivan gave in on this point, but it was not long before he was picking holes in Gilbert's libretto. Indeed, he found so many faults with the second act that Gilbert's patience finally gave out, and he exclaimed testily: "Well, write the confounded music first, and I'll fit the words afterward!"

"All right, I will!" Sullivan shouted back defiantly, realizing full well that Gilbert had not intended his challenge to be taken seriously.

After an infuriating delay of several weeks, Gilbert received the music from Sullivan, and settled to his difficult task of fitting the words to the tune. He found this technique extremely burdensome and was greatly disgruntled with the result of his labors. On dispatching the verses to Sullivan, he enclosed a tart note, saying, "It is mere doggerel, but words written to an existing tune are nearly sure to be that . . . Chop the stuff about as much as you like. I don't mind what you do with it."

Clearly, neither Gilbert nor Sullivan could get his heart into this opera. As Gilbert had warned Chappell, the sympathetic understanding that had inspired *The Mikado, H.M.S. Pinafore,* and all the others in their long chain of successes, had been broken beyond repair.

The opening performance of *Utopia Limited,* on October 7, 1893, had a heartening reception, the audience bursting into thunderous applause and repeatedly calling Gilbert and Sullivan before the curtain. After Gilbert and Sullivan had taken the first few calls separately from opposite wings, the audience insisted upon their appearing together as proof that their quarrel was really over and forgotten. "Author *and* composer—Gilbert *and* Sullivan!" they shouted as with one voice. Sullivan, who was offstage awaiting his turn, played up to them by striding to the center, smiling genially, and shaking Gilbert warmly by the hand. As the curtain fell on the two men, clasped in apparent friendship, the audience clapped, stamped their feet, and shouted themselves hoarse.

But their mad acclaim was generated only by their pleasure at seeing the partners reunited; it gave no indication of their feelings for the opera itself. Neither the theatergoers nor the critics considered *Utopia Limited* as comparable to the earlier operas, and it was withdrawn after only a few months.

For the next three years the partners again went their separate ways, until in 1896, when Gilbert was fifty-nine and Sullivan fifty-four, D'Oyly Carte, after persistent pleading, persuaded them to collaborate in one more opera, *The Grand Duke*. They were persuaded against their own better judgment, agreeing to undertake the work simply out of a mistaken sense of loyalty to D'Oyly Carte. The result, therefore, was inevitable: *The Grand Duke*, their last opera, was a dismal failure.

And so, the most famous, and possibly the most successful, partnership in theatrical history ended.

Sullivan now tried to restore his declining health and shattered nerves by undergoing medicinal treatment at various well-known health centers on the Continent, one "cure" consisting of drinking six pints of mineral water before breakfast and then spending the rest of the day with alternate massage and baths. This "taking the waters," as it was called, proved as ineffective as all his other treatments: his kidney disease was slowly killing him.

For weeks on end, Sullivan would lie prostrate on his bed, too weak even to read, but then, feeling suddenly better, he would bounce back to life and indulge in all the social activities that had come to mean so much to him—going to the races, gambling at Monte Carlo, riding in Hyde Park's fashionable Rotten Row, and hobnobbing with royalty. He went to stay, from time to time, with several members of the royal family. This included paying a visit to Windsor Castle as the guest of the Queen, to celebrate whose Diamond Jubilee, in 1897, he was commissioned to compose another work that received Her Majesty's usual rich approval. He also paid several visits to foreign royalty.

With his American friend, Mrs. Ronalds, now his constant companion, doing the duty of hostess, Sullivan did a good deal of entertaining by giving elaborate dinner parties for his aristocratic friends. The Prince and Princess of Wales and the Duke and Duchess of Edinburgh dined at his house on several occasions. After dinner, Mrs. Ronalds, who had a rich contralto voice, would sing them some of Sullivan's songs to his own accompaniment, the favorite being *The Lost Chord*.

Though seldom out of pain, Sullivan managed to compose a variety of works during these last four years of his life. And on November 17, 1898 he made his last appearance at The Savoy to conduct the orchestra at a revival of *The Sorcerer*, staged in celebration of the twenty-first anniversary of the original production. At the end of the performance, the audience shouted for Gilbert and Sullivan, in the hope that again they might shake hands on the stage, as after *Utopia Limited*. But they were disappointed. Tense and expressionless, Gilbert and Sullivan walked onto the stage from opposite wings, and, keeping their distance, bowed formally. They then returned to their respective wings with neither a word nor even a smile for each other. They never met again.

In September 1900, while staying in Switzerland grappling with a new composition, Sullivan was drenched to the skin in a severe storm on his way to lunch with a royal visitor to that country. He contracted bronchitis, and, his constitution being weak, this hastened his death. Returning home as soon as he was in a fit condition to travel, he lingered on for another two months in the care of his faithful valet, Louis Jager.

One day Jager was unable to restrain his tears as he bent over his dying master. Sullivan, understanding the reason for his sorrow, smiled and said in a feeble voice: "Why do you cry? I am perfectly happy and contented.

You must not cry for me. How do you think I could be otherwise than happy when I am going to see my dear mother?"

In the late afternoon of November 21, Sullivan's strength began to fail and a second doctor was called in for consultation. After the doctors had attended to him, Sullivan rallied a little and passed a peaceful night. But at six o'clock next morning, the 22nd, his valet and his nephew Herbert, who had been summoned by the doctors, were awakened by the violent ringing of his bell. As they rushed into his bedroom, Sullivan struggled to sit up, gasping: "My heart! My heart!"

Herbert calmed his uncle as best he could and instructed the valet to telephone immediately for Mrs. Ronalds and the Prince of Wales's physician. But it was too late: Sullivan died in his nephew's arms before they could reach him.

Sir Arthur Sullivan, who was only fifty-eight, had expressed a wish to be buried in the same grave as his father, mother and brother; but, at the personal request of the Queen, he was given a hero's funeral in St. Paul's Cathedral, following a service at the Chapel Royal, where he had trained as a chorister.

D'Oyly Carte was by now gravely ill, so ill that the doctors ordered the news of Sullivan's death to be kept from him. However, as the funeral procession passed his home in Adelphi Terrace, some instinct made him rise from his sickbed and look out of the window. An hour or so later, he was found on the floor in a state of collapse. "I have just seen the last of my old friend Sullivan," he said, his eyes filled with tears. Within six months, D'Oyly Carte followed Sullivan to the grave.

Gilbert was in Egypt, trying to cure his crippling gout by a change of climate, at the time of Sullivan's death, and the first intimation he received of the tragedy was a bald announcement in a newspaper, which he happened to read by pure chance. He was deeply shocked.

"I remember," he remarked remorsefully, "all he has done for me in allowing his genius to shed some of its luster upon my humble name."

Later, Gilbert paid Sullivan another tribute that summarizes the secret of their many and brilliant successes: "We always saw eye to eye. The same humor always struck us in exactly the same way. With Sullivan, I never had to do that fatal thing—explain a joke."

CHAPTER FIFTEEN

Gilbert's Last Years

Gilbert, who survived Sullivan by between ten and eleven years, spent the remainder of his life living like a country squire at Harrow Weald, a district which, though now a suburb of London, was then in the heart of the countryside.

During the tragic years of his quarrel with Sullivan, he had sold his London house and bought himself a large mock Tudor house, Grim's Dyke, standing in 110 acres of rolling well-wooded grounds.

Delighted to have left the hustle and bustle of London after his strenuous years in the theater, Gilbert spent a fortune on developing the grounds, stocking the garden with colorful flowering shrubs and planting a lawn as perfect as a bowling green. He started a small farm, laid out fruit and vegetable gardens that became the envy of his neighbors, and, perhaps his greatest pride, also constructed a large lake where he could bathe when his rheumatism and gout permitted.

The Gilberts, who by now had adopted an actress, Nancy McIntosh, as their daughter, had to employ a staff of twenty servants to maintain this property, eight to run the house and twelve for the upkeep of the farms and gardens, and all this for just three people.

But the Gilberts never lacked companions. As devoted to animals as to children, they surrounded themselves with cats and dogs and treated them all like human beings. At mealtimes, cats and dogs alike would be shepherded into the dining room (where a separate tablecloth had been laid on the floor for each animal) to dine in state with their master and mistress. Each pet had its appointed chair or basket downstairs where it might sleep during the daytime and a more luxurious bed upstairs for the nighttime. Before retiring for the night, Gilbert would give each cat and dog a small toy to take to bed with it, and, with these in their mouths, they would follow him in procession up the stairs to their respective sleeping quarters.

Gilbert also made pets of several other species of animal. He kept a number of monkeys, a pair of lemurs, a fallow deer, and a donkey whose bray was so high-pitched that he nicknamed her Adelina after the famous operatic singer, Adelina Patti. Every few months he seemed to acquire some new animal, until the place was like a menagerie.

These numerous animals would wander freely in and out of the ever open French windows leading into Gilbert's library, two of his most frequent visitors being Adelina, the donkey, and the little fallow deer, which were inseparable friends. As Gilbert sat in his chair reading, the deer would burrow her nose into his lap to indicate that she and Adelina wished to be taken for a walk—a request that Gilbert always found difficult to refuse. Dressed in his country tweeds, he would walk them along the lanes and over the fields with the donkey ambling along on one side of him and the deer frisking on the other.

One day the deer became more venturesome and started to jump the hedges. Finding that the donkey could not follow her example, she showed off and soon got quite out of hand. During the next few weeks, she ran wild, causing so much damage to the neighbors' crops that eventually Gilbert, unwilling to pay for any more of her mischief, took her to a park and let her loose among a herd of wild deer. A year or so later, while walking in this same park, Gilbert saw the herd at a distance and gave a whistle. Immediately the deer broke away from the herd and bounced toward him. Not long afterward, she sniffed her way back to Gilbert's library, and he had not the heart to turn her away again.

Gilbert felt a particular affection for the pair of lemurs, which he had imported from Madagascar. The first time he allowed them into his library they spluttered at his cigar smoke, jumped onto his shoulder, pulled the offending cigar from his mouth and threw it onto the floor. Gradually, however, they grew to appreciate the aroma and made a habit of sitting on the arms of his chair, one on each side, and inhaling the whiffs as he smoked. The lemurs often caused havoc in both house and grounds, helping themselves to food from the dining table and running riot in the fruit garden, but Gilbert could never bring himself to punish them.

Then one day they atoned for all their mischief. "A most interesting occurrence in our household!" Gilbert wrote jubilantly in his diary. "A baby, quite unexpectedly, has been born—to whom do you think?—to our two lemurs! It is the rarest possible thing for ring-tailed lemurs to breed in captivity."

Gilbert also kept a number of parrots, all of which were allowed the same freedom as the rest of his pets. Seldom caged, they had a habit of flying into the dining room when guests were present, causing amusement and occasionally embarrassment by swearing or breaking into ribald laughter.

Not content with his parrots, Gilbert tamed birds from the fields and hedgerow, training them to eat out of his hand, and scattering nesting boxes in various parts of the house to encourage them to breed in comfort and luxury. He began by tempting robins, bullfinches and pigeons into his library, but it was not long before cranes and other giants of bird life were taking advantage of his hospitality. Finally, half a dozen plump turkeys from the farm, refusing to be left in the cold, strutted in and sat themselves down on his sofa and chairs.

Gilbert once tamed a bee that flew in through his window. He nicknamed the bee "Buzfuz," fed it daily on sugar, and coaxed it to sleep each night in a box in a corner of the room.

Animals, birds and even insects were always sure of a welcome, but human beings had a more mixed reception.

"Tell the man to go to the devil!" Gilbert roared when one day his butler gingerly poked his head around the door and announced that a newspaper reporter had called to see him.

The butler, accustomed to these outbursts, discreetly withdrew and delivered the message in rather more polite terms: "Mr. Gilbert is very sorry, but he wishes me to state that extreme pressure of work must deny him the pleasure of seeing you this morning."

Gilbert experienced great difficulty in being civil to reporters. One stout woman reporter, to whom he had granted admittance only with the greatest reluctance, tried to humor him by making an exaggerated fuss over his dogs. "Dear, sweet, delightful creatures!" she kept repeating as four or five of them endeavored to clamber onto her lap. "It is wonderful how dogs always seem to take to me immediately."

Gilbert glanced her up and down and ungallantly retorted: "Not at all, madam! It is not often they get a bone to pick with so much meat upon it!"

His dislike of reporters stemmed from his complete inability to accept the smallest criticism of his work. Gilbert had always been so sensitive on this point that throughout his partnership with Sullivan his wife had tried to scan his reviews to make sure they were "inoffensive" before Gilbert could get hold of them, and had made a practice of hiding or destroying any likely to send him into a tantrum. Unfortunately, she could not always be the first to see the reviews. On one occasion, Gilbert, while turning the pages of a magazine, came upon a general article about himself, with a heading implying that it was not complimentary. He read on: "Mr. Gilbert's abnormal self-esteem has, with advancing years, developed into a malady. In his own estimation he is a kind of Grand Lama or Sacred Elephant of dramatic literature. The mildest criticism of his work, the most gentle disapproval of one of his plays, is a crime for which, if it were in his power, he would punish the culprit severely."

There was only one answer to this sort of insult, Gilbert decided: he promptly sued the editor for libel, claiming £1,000 ($5,000) damages.

During the hearing of his case, Gilbert was challenged by counsel for the defense: "You do not like reading hostile criticism?"

"I have a horror of reading criticism at all, either good or bad," he replied. When counsel tried to extract an admission that, in fact, it was only the bad of which he had a horror, Gilbert protested that, on the contrary, he considered the unfavorable reviews the lesser of the two evils. He added impishly: "I know how good I am, but I do *not* know how bad I am!"

At this, there was general laughter. Gilbert caused more amusement when, in further cross-examination, he described a popular pantomime as "bad musical comedy, in which half a dozen irresponsible comedians are turned loose on the stage to do as they please."

"Would you really describe a pantomime as a bad musical comedy?" defending counsel pressed him.

"No," Gilbert flashed, "but I would describe a bad musical comedy as a pantomime!"

The action developed into a battle of wits in which Gilbert was always supreme. Wit, however, was not sufficient to prove libel; and, after an absence of nearly three hours, the jury failed to reach agreement, and the case was dismissed.

During his long and successful career as a librettist, Gilbert had taken legal action, often upon the flimsiest pretext, against numerous people with whom he had "disagreed."

His friends used to say jokingly that he must have spent almost as much time in the witness box as at the theater. Certainly the actions he brought kept him far busier than the briefs he had received as a lawyer.

Having indulged in litigation for most of his working life, Gilbert spent his last years serving as a magistrate. The High Sheriff of Middlesex, when interviewing him for this appointment, remarked inquiringly: "You have, I believe, studied law, and have a sound knowledge of the subject?"

"That is so," Gilbert replied with a twinkle in his eye, "but I hope you will not consider this an impediment!"

As a magistrate, Gilbert displayed the same spirit of independence as he had always shown in the theater, combining severity with extreme kindness. In his determination always to be scrupulously fair to the accused, he was apt to place more reliance upon the evidence of the prisoner in the dock than upon the testimony of the police appearing for the prosecution. And, if a man was convicted by a majority decision of the court for a crime of which he personally considered him innocent, Gilbert would take his fellow magistrates to task, and sometimes follow this up with more drastic action.

Once, when a man was sentenced to a fine or imprisonment on a charge of assault, of which, in Gilbert's opinion, he had not been proved guilty, Gilbert immediately paid the man's fine out of his own pocket. He made formal protest to the Chairman of the Bench by letter, threatening that in future, rather than be a party to another miscarriage of justice, he would "take the course of publicly disclaiming concurrence with your decision."

When Gilbert himself presided over the court, he frequently took the unusual step of investigating the background and circumstances of the accused before they were brought before him. When judging their cases, he would be strictly impartial, keeping within the letter of the law and fitting the punishment to the crime; but, when he had occasion to impose a fine that was likely to cause undue hardship to the accused's family, he would call on the victim later in the day and secretly give him the money to settle his fine, with a warning that if he repeated the offense he would be sent to prison.

But, though Gilbert always gave the accused the benefit of the doubt, and did his best to avoid causing hardship to the poor, he nevertheless would show no mercy to anyone whose social background made his crime inexcusable. Once, when an aristocratic young man whom he had sentenced to prison for some minor offense announced his intention to appeal to the Home Secretary, Gilbert fixed him with his penetrating eye and told him gruffly: "You will serve your sentence whatever the Home Secretary may say!" The man withdrew his notice of appeal and went to prison.

Gilbert was particularly severe on motorists. Motoring was then in its infancy, and cars were still considered highly unsafe: unless the greatest care were taken, engines were liable to explode, tires to burst, or the vehicle to turn over. Anyone driving at a speed above about twenty miles an hour along those narrow, twisting lanes, designed for horses, was regarded as a lunatic, and likely to run into trouble with the police. Cases of "speeding" constantly came before Gilbert, and he meted out such heavy penalties that the culprits took care not to exceed the limit a second time within the area of his jurisdiction.

It was, perhaps, surprising that Gilbert should have been so firm with motorists, for his own experiences as a car-owner were most unfortunate. During his first few years at Harrow, Gilbert used to drive around the countryside in a carriage drawn by a pair of horses which he called "Bryant and May," but in the early 1900's, when motoring began to increase in popularity, he bought himself a large American steam car, a chugging monster that became the terror of the district.

"I made my début," Gilbert tells us, "by spoiling a parson, who came round from under a wall on a bicycle. He was pretty badly hurt. The car was turned over at a ditch. I was pitched over the dashboard onto my head (I saw stars of beautiful colors and was quite sorry when they vanished), and my wife was pitched very comfortably into a hedge, where she looked like a large and quite unaccountable bird's nest."

A few weeks later, while on an outing to Chesham, he had a second calamity. "Although we were only creeping on at two miles an hour, we caused a horse, which was driven in a trap by two ladies, to shy up a bank. The trap was all but capsized. One lady was thrown out and run over; the groom was also thrown out, and the trap went over his hand; the horse then bolted with the other lady, who was eventually stopped without damage. Happily, the lady who was run over was not much hurt. . . ."

Gilbert accepted no responsibility for these accidents, nor for others to follow, and thought motoring highly delectable.

Though he spent most of his time in the country, Gilbert did not desert the theater entirely. He built the Garrick Theatre; discovered and encouraged several young actors and actresses who later were to make their name, one being Ellaline Terris who became one of the most famous actresses of her day; and from time to time supervised revivals of the Savoy operas. He did very little writing, however. "I have been scribbling twaddle for thirty-five years, and I am about sick of it. I shouldn't mind if I never wrote another word," he told a friend.

Indeed, he wrote so little, and appeared in public so seldom after Sullivan's death that one critic assumed him to be also dead and referred to him in a newspaper article as "the late W. S. Gilbert"—a slip which Gilbert saw fit to correct by advising the editor: "There is a line in your issue of yesterday that must have sent a thrill of joy through many a worthy home . . . I am always sorry to spoil sport, but common candor compels me to admit (reluctantly) that I am still alive."

In July 1907, at the age of seventy, Gilbert at last received the recognition that had been due to him for so long: he was offered a knighthood by King Edward VII who, as the Prince of Wales, had been such a close friend of Sullivan's. It was now twenty-four years since Sullivan had received the same honor, and Gilbert, much as he had envied his partner at the time, no longer felt any desire for this "tin-pot, two-penny-halfpenny sort of distinction." However, he decided to accept the title because, as he said, "as no dramatic author as such ever had it for dramatic authorship alone, I felt I ought not to refuse it."

He set off for Buckingham Palace to receive his knight-hood in a most disgruntled mood, almost as though he were doing the King a favor by accepting the honor; and when later a woman acquaintance addressed him, half in jest, as "Sir William," he turned on her, and ordered: "Call me Bill!"

Gilbert enjoyed his old age. "My experience," he re-marked to a friend, "is that old age is the happiest time in a man's life. The worst of it is there's so little of it." His happiest hours were those spent in his garden, pottering among the flower beds, ambling down to the farm, indulg-ing in a placid game of croquet with a guest or neighbor, reading Dickens or Trollope under the shade of a tree, or, better than anything, swimming in his lake. "I hope that, when my time comes, I may die upon a summer's day in my own garden," he told his friend.

His wish was fulfilled.

Five days later, on May 29, 1911, a perfect day with the sun shining from a clear blue sky, Gilbert, now seventy-four, went to London to attend some morning function; he lunched at his club, where he patched up a quarrel with an actor with whom he had not been on speaking terms for some twenty years; and then he caught an early-afternoon train home again.

He arrived back in high spirits, looking forward to a prearranged swim in his lake with two girls, Winifred and Ruby, who lived nearby.

"I'll just go up and change. I shan't be a minute," he told them.

While he was changing, the girls sauntered down to the lake and plunged in. Alas, neither Winifred nor Ruby could swim very well. Finding herself out of her depth, Ruby panicked and shouted to Winifred for assistance. As Winifred was struggling to reach her, Gilbert, having heard Ruby's scream and hurried his pace, arrived at the lake.

"Don't be frightened!" he shouted. "It's not very deep. You'll be all right. Hold on—I'm coming!"

Gilbert dived in and swam to her rescue. "Now then," he spluttered on reaching her, "just put your hands on my shoulders, and don't struggle."

Ruby did as he told her, and floated to safety. But, when she and Winifred clambered ashore and looked back across the lake, they could see no sign of Gilbert. Their screams of anguish brought a gardener running to the scene. He hurriedly unmoored the boat and went in search of his master, but, though he quickly recovered his body, he could not save his life.

The exertion of trying to swim ashore with Ruby on his shoulder had given Gilbert a fatal heart attack. He had died, as he hoped he would, in his own garden, in the lake that was his pride.

Only a few days before his tragic death, Gilbert had remarked wistfully: "I fancy that posterity will know as little of me as I shall of posterity." How wrong he was.

BIBLIOGRAPHY

Sir Arthur Sullivan by A. Lawrence (London, 1899)

Sir Arthur Sullivan by B. W. Findon (London, 1904)

W. S. Gilbert by S. Dark and R. Grey (Doran, 1923)

Arthur Seymour Sullivan by H. Saxe Wyndham (Harper, 1926)

Gilbert and Sullivan and D'Oyly Carte by F. Cellier and C. Bridgeman (Pitman, 1927)

The Story of Gilbert and Sullivan by I. Goldberg (Simon and Schuster, 1928)

Gilbert and Sullivan by H. Pearson (Harper, 1935)

Gilbert by H. Pearson (Harper, 1958)

Sir Arthur Sullivan by H. Sullivan and Sir N. Flower (Cassell, 1950)

The Gilbert and Sullivan Book by L. Baily (Cassell, 1952)

Training the Gilbert and Sullivan Chorus by W. Cox-Ife (Chappell, 1955)